A
Good Life

John Seymour and his
self-sufficiency legacy

By Paul Peacock

" I am only one.
I can only do what one can do.
But what one can do, I will do! "

John Seymour (1914-2004)

Published 2005

ISBN 1904871-12-7

A catalogue record for this book is available from
the British Library.

Published by
Farming Books and Videos Ltd.
PO Box 536
Preston
PR2 9ZY
www.farmingbooksandvideos.com

Cover design by Rebecca Peacock
Pen and Ink drawings by Rebecca Peacock

Produced and set by Farming Books and Videos Ltd
Printed and bound in Great Britain by Mackays of Chatham plc

Contents

Acknowledgements

There are many people to thank for their invaluable assistance in the writing of this book. There were dozens of people who helped with anecdotes and archive material, in particular Anne and David Sears have not only given long suffering help in checking facts, but have warmly welcomed my wife Diana and myself into their home and have become great friends.

Sally Seymour and her sister, Diana, have provided both information and inspiration, for which I am truly grateful and my publisher, Ruth Tott and her husband Paul, who have provided welcome support.

Many thanks go to Rebecca Peacock for her illustrations and wise words about the manuscripts, without which the work would still remain unfinished.

Of course my love and thanks go to Diana, Rebecca, Joshua and Joel for putting up with me during the long gestation of this work.

Introduction

Anyone born into the twentieth century will have experienced a great deal of change throughout the course of their lives. The economies, politics and cultures of the world have altered so much during the ninety odd years from the beginning of the First World War, that people of John Seymour's generation would have experienced more change than any other humans in history. Throughout all this John Seymour had been a student of people and their cultures. Of course, much more than that, he was a champion of self sufficiency, of green politics, of literature, travel and, foremost, a lover of life itself, for which he had a huge appetite. Essentially, however, John was a lover of people, their lives and their relationships.

He fought against those forces that are at work in the world intent on mass uniformity; acres of monoculture, genetically modified crops, systems of distribution and banking, monopolies and the impoverishment of humanity in the modern world. All have been antagonised by John with an often violent passion. In one way or another various institutions, banks, governments and multinational companies have forced people from the land into a life where the vital skills they had inherited from generations past, skills that enable them to prosper in wonderfully diverse ways, seem now to be moribund and derided. John's life was a drive to preserve these skills as he knew that one day they would be needed again.

John's common sense way of recording the lives of ordinary people; African bushmen, Birmingham barge men, long forgotten real gypsies, poverty bound Indian farmers, fishermen, soldiers, poachers, beggars, is matched by his appetite for the knowledge and skills that made them what they were. This book is a celebration of John Seymour, his life journey and some of the people he met and loved along the way. We shall share in the events of his life, take a look into his philosophy and finally take up the gauntlet of his battle cry;

> " *I am only one.*
> *I can only do what one can do.*
> *But what one can do I will do!* "

How can you write a book about a man who has lived for nearly a century and achieved so much? Even worse, how can you write a book about a man whose life is not only so diverse, but also quite difficult to understand at times?

Ever since I read *The Fat of the Land* I had considered myself his friend. More desperate a friend he never had. Reading *The Fat of the Land* brought to me a companion who was living out a life of which I had only dreamed. If John could do it, why not me? As the chapters introduced some new aspect of life at the Broom (John and Sally's first smallholding) I became entranced. The book came into my possession at a low point for me. The city life I was living was becoming unbearable and it was a personal solace each evening to bury my head into the pages and simply dream.

John meant so much to so many different people. In my ignorant way, having only read one of his books, (back to back and constantly for a year not withstanding) I felt I had a picture of the man. But as one swallow does not make a summer, one book is not a real image of a man. It took many years to glean John's real heart, his deep concern for the planet, his deeper concern for people, and his ability to love outrageously with a certain style and deep sincerity.

This book, consequently, is about John. Not his wives, his children or his friends, though you find some of them here. More specifically it is about his thinking and how his life philosophy was borne out of his experiences. Not everyone who would consider themselves a close friend of John or his family are included in this book simply because it is centred on the man's mind, not his friends. Of course, it is not really possible to write about a person and miss out all the facts of his life from year to year and so you will find some important characters, but not all. Some of you will cry,

'How can one write a book about John Seymour and not mention so and so?' and for that you have my condolences, but not my apologies. It has never been my intention to write about his lifestyle or his choices, preferring to stick with his thinking. Fortunately nearly all of John's writings are auto-biographical in one way or another and you could do no better than to refer to his books for the willy-nilly and the nitty-gritty.

Paul Peacock

Manchester, June 2005

Author's Note: One of the problems a biographer has is what to call his subject: Mr Seymour, Captain Seymour, John Seymour, John? I chose John Seymour for formality, but where it was necessary, simply John for friendliness. Needless to say, there is a lot more of friendliness than formality in this book.

Chapter One
The Real Life

Albert Angus Turbayne was born in Boston,
Massachusetts in 1866. He was a successful
artist and book designer. At the turn of the century
he was quite prolific producing wood cut typefaces, monograms and ciphers and a title called *The
Beautiful Birthday Book*. His drawn alphabets were
the first modern collection of typefaces ever made.
They still have importance today and are in use by
a subsidiary of Microsoft in the manufacture of
fonts. He was a member of the Carlton Studio of
Designers and Illustrators which boasted the im-
posing address of 180 Fleet Street and his seminal
work regularly sells at auction for over a hundred
pounds. He won a bronze medal for binding design
at the Paris 1900 Exhibition. He had many suc-
cesses in his professional life and many failures in

his personal one. He appears to have been not too good with drink, not too good with money and not too good being married to Christiana.

Christiana had given birth to William in 1911 and then John in 1914 and, shortly after, the relationship between husband and wife broke down. By this time Albert was already fifty years old and his considerably younger wife had enough energy to throw herself into new relationships and another marriage. She had taken herself and the boys to 'The Manor', the home of Albert Angus Turbayne's uncle, William Angus, leaving her husband 'up garret' as John put it, in London. The Manor was in Essex, seven miles from Frinton-on-Sea.

Curtain Road in Shoreditch had, since the turn of the eighteenth century, been the centre of furniture manufacture in London. William Angus's factory was there, nestled with dozens of others. His mass-produced furniture was sold in the growing cities around the country and he was very successful for many years. There was a great need for good quality but affordable furniture and Uncle William was well established in the industry. His income grew, to such a point that he was able to buy The Manor as his home. Here he played the country gentleman, but without shooting or fishing.

The boys were very happy there, John in particular, spending his time with the 'low life', a class of people with whom he came to have a particular affinity. The term low life did not have the same connotations that it has today, but meant tradesmen, servants, gardeners and farm workers; the servile classes. John preferred to spend his early days in their company. They were warm people, caring and interesting.

Christiana's character is drawn by John as a combination of drama and falsity. He describes her as a woman who enjoyed playing parts. She loved the role of 'Lady of the Manor', into which she threw herself. She entertained Uncle William's guests, ran the household (which amounted to a five minute conversation about food with the cook) and socialised with the 'Bright Young Things' of Frinton-on-Sea. With the outbreak of war she entertained officers, giving balls each week, drove them around the country and put up selected officers who had been wounded at the front line so they could convalesce. Frequently gentlemen officers of the Flying Corps, later the RAF, would land their machines in the field next to The Manor. One of John's earliest memories was of being lifted up to see inside the cockpit. He writes about the time as being one in which he was uncomfortable, neither particularly happy or unhappy. But children know when they are loved and he felt more at home in the kitchen, not the dining room; with the cook, not the family.

John spent his early 'playing out' days up trees or wandering around the countryside, for

which he was developing a deep love. He was
fished out of the lake on several occasions, once by
local gypsies, other times by his brother. He fell
out of trees and was generally very happy doing all
the things that young boys do. He followed the
farm workers around or pestered the chauffeur and
was entertained by the servants while doing their
duties. His favourite pass-time was getting them to
sing songs to him such as 'Chase me Charley' and
'The little Grey Home in the West'. John said that
these people were more real to him than his own
family, and perhaps this, among others, is the reason why he remained closer to what he would describe as real working people than any other section of society all his life.

The idea of what was *real* would follow him
through his life. To modern people the word real
has lost some of its meaning. For John, playing the
rich boy was important because that's all he then
knew but it was not *real*. His encounter with servants who had to work for their keep was *real*, it
was vital and the attitudes they showed about life
were vital also. As John grew up the choice between kitchen and dining room was an easy one. In
the dining room you had to pretend, in the kitchen
you could be yourself.

John's natural father was absent. He had no
contact save for a single letter. John wrote to him
at the office of a publisher for whom he was the
Art Editor, and the response was non-committal

and disappointing. When John wrote *On My Own Terms* in 1963 he did not know if his father was dead or alive. Albert Angus Turbayne actually died in 1940 in London, having retired from the London County Council School of Photoengraving and Lithography.

Certainly, his mother was, at best, distant. She was an important figure in his youth, but their relationship could not be described as warm; she was far too busy making a life for herself in the well to do world of The Manor. She persuaded Uncle William to get himself a house in London on the pretext that he could use it when in town. In actual fact he always stayed at his club, and Christiana, the two boys and a few servants ended up living in St. John's Wood in expensive furnished accommodation. Mother was, as John put it, "*hell bent on making a really impressive marriage.*" And she did. She had an affinity for High Society in the same measure as John's for servants and farm workers, gypsies and the like. She associated with princes and social climbers in a world of dances and clubs and high pranks. By all accounts she had a number of suitors, and of them she chose Tom.

Tom is a commonplace name for a very exclusive man. Like her first husband he, too, was an American and a very rich one at that. Thomas Seymour was the great-grandson of one of the founders of the oatmeal giant Quaker Oats. He moved to London to head up the UK and European opera-

tion and, exploiting the age of advertising, Quaker
Oats had quickly become the leading breakfast
manufacturer in the country. In 1922 they produced 'Quick Oats,' an almost instant porridge
which out sold every other product on the market.
This was more than enough to make Tom Seymour
very rich indeed. He became stepfather and eventually 'Pater' to John and his brother, and a never
ending source of funds and social experiences for
their mother. Many years later, John asked his
mother why she married Thomas Seymour. She
made it clear that she did so because it was obvious
that he was 'going to be a millionaire.' This did not
impress, and clearly John had inherited his natural
father's inclination with regards to money. He may
have earned a lot during his life time, but he was to
prove himself unable to hang on to it.

Thomas Seymour was adamant that he was
not going to pay for an English education for the
boys. However, Uncle William stood by his neph-
ews. The finances he saved by not having to provide a London home for Christiana and family following the divorce from Albert Turbayne, was
spent on an expensive education at a boarding prep
school for the boys.

William and John were sent away from home
to learn prayers and Latin and the general degrada-
tion of life in an expensive establishment populated
by a mix of 'heartless' staff and 'snobbish little
brats'. In school John found the lack of privacy dif-

ficult to deal with. For a boy like John, who was determined not to engage either in sport or learning, it was a long and difficult period.

John's brother, Bill, was a high flyer. William Seymour had a capacity for learning that John not only admired, but later emulated. In the holidays they would discuss literature, science and the arts together. They would read avidly, so much so that their schooling was of secondary importance. They were somewhat different in nature, John and Bill. John was much less conventional, he refused to show his learning in school, he refused to join in sports, actually doing badly whenever he could. Bill was more of a school hero, out-classing all the rest academically. Bill came top in class, John came bottom. Eventually Bill became a leading Civil Servant and the boys drifted apart in later life. When Bill died, John did not hear of it, and sadly he was not invited to the funeral.

When Uncle William died the funds for schooling died with him. John and Bill were sent to day school, and even with his great wealth, 'Pater' stuck to his word and did not find money enough for their education. Their mother paid for their schooling out of her own funds, granted they were funds provided by her husband, but they were hers none the less. A succession of house moves finally found John at Frinton-on-Sea again and set up as a day boy at the Valley School. Here he consistently came bottom in everything. He daydreamed himself through his early teens, imagining things like knights in shining armour, pirate ships or American cowboys. The only thing he excelled at was shooting, at which he was invariably top of the school.

John did not like his home, Tudor House, in the exclusive part of the town. He described everything as ostentatious, expensive and vulgar. His parents spent a lot of money simply for show; the newest plants for the front garden, big cars, antique furniture and all the trappings of wealth. John's mother had the front hedge pulled out so that people walking past could see into the garden and up to the house. They spent a fortune extending the property, adding extra bedrooms and whole wings. John did, however, enjoy the Essex countryside. He got to know every hedge, field and stream as he sallied around the place, dreaming of adventures, climbing the cliffs, hiding while watching farm workers or road men, trying to spend a whole day without being seen by anyone. Along with Bill he considered himself a naturalist, and collected beetles, butterflies and fossils from all over the area. Because of his love for natural history, his mother marked him to become a doctor but deep down inside he really wanted to be a cowboy.

John's love for cowboys made him want to be American. He was legally of dual, possibly triple nationality. His natural father had American and Canadian nationality, and John was determined that, when he was twenty-one, he would opt for American nationality. He even had a picture of George Washington above his bed. America symbolised rebellion and adventure - the very things he found difficult to resist all his life. This made him his stepfather's ally in the home when it came to questions of nationality and race. And yet, in reality, John's relationship with 'Pater' was not that good. He was preferred over his brother, but this did not impress him at all. John referred to him as vulgar, not interested in anyone other than himself; a nationalistic bully who would not take on board anyone else's culture or language. Thomas Seymour was said to hate people who were 'doers' - preferring himself to be a 'buyer'. He would not learn French, even though he was the managing director of the French arm of Quaker Oats, because he could pay someone to translate what was said in the boardroom for him. He didn't drive because he could pay someone to drive for him. He scoffed at all forms of art and this rubbed off on his wife. But, almost rebelliously, John cultured a love of classical music, of art, architecture and reading.

Perhaps because he was older and perhaps because he was not 'Pater's' favourite, Bill cultivated a staunchly English demeanour, antagonising his stepfather at any and every opportunity. When Bill was twenty one he threw away his American passport and became the archetypal Englishman.

John had been sent to public school where he sank deeper into Bunyan's 'Slough of Despond', finding it to be a heartless, loveless place. He made plans to run away and wrote pitiful letters home. Eventually they paid off. He was finally removed from school when, during a visit by his mother, he announced in front of the Head Teacher that if she did not remove him from the awful place he would run away. It worked, and John was sent away to 'La Clairiere,' a school in Switzerland. Bill had been sent there largely as a consequence of his failing health or more possibly to get him out of the house and from under 'Pater's' feet. John describes this move as being transferred from "Purgatory to Paradise". He loved the walks, the nature and the outdoors.

From La Clairiere he moved to the highly regarded Institute Silig. Situated on the banks of Lake Geneva this school was full of Americans and Theodore Roosevelt had been educated there. John became great friends with the American pupils and thoroughly loved it. He learned French and for the first time in his school years he became popular.

A friendship with an American boy strengthened John's desire to become a cowboy then a rancher, an altogether more acceptable occupation for a child of such parents. His world in Europe was privileged and wealthy and very happy until he started to hanker for what he called real, low life people. He came to see this time as a *"strange, useless, completely pointless life; but lived intensely."*

There were many train journeys across Europe back to England and then back to Switzerland and school. To make such a trip might seem unsafe for a teenager these days but to John travelling was commonplace. He was to become a journeyman; tasting the different cultures and writing about what he found.

His desire to become a cowboy/rancher prompted his mother to place him in Agricultural College, so his last trip from Switzerland was, much to his chagrin, to rejoin his countrymen almost for good. He was enrolled in the South Eastern Agricultural College at Wye in Kent, but first had to get hands on experience for six months. He reported for duty at the farm of Mr Catt in Feering, Essex.

Moving to the farm was the biggest shock of his life. Up by candlelight and at work by six in the morning, his first job was to check and feed the stock. Cattle and pigs were his responsibility and offered a real contrast to his Swiss education which he enjoyed.

After breakfast each morning he was faced with eight hours hoeing. Working in a team, a line of men took every weed out of the fields and hoed through the day. When the pain in his muscles decreased, the boredom levels increased.

It was the hardest work he had ever known but he felt he was able to face his middle class parent's knowing they knew nothing of the lot of what they called 'idle workmen'.

Although the work was hard he stuck at it and eventually even enjoyed its physical side. He said that he found out something new; the glory of the companionship of men when they were working together. His acceptance by the other men, after a time of learning and strengthening up, increased his own self-esteem and he grew because of it. More than anything he found what was always latent within him; a great love for country people, old fashioned country ways and, above all, the way the ordinary folk managed to eek out a living from the land. This was the *real life* he was looking for.

He says he found a new ethos, and its discovery rendered the old world of fine houses, money, cars, servants and status absolutely valueless. He thought of food not in terms of money but in relation to toil and sweat, and he discovered that labour; hard, strenuous and continued labour that made a man perspire freely, was better than any sport he knew. John believed 'a healthy mind and a healthy body', the stated aim of all sports, was gained, not by chasing a ball around, but by *"digging or ploughing or hoeing or laying bricks or fishing."*

His new found ideas about the countryside

and country people led both to his success and his failure at Wye College. He described himself as bone idle, but of course he was far from it. What he meant was that he didn't like studying. He preferred the outdoors to the indoors of the lecture room and, although he was really good at practical subjects such as veterinary science, he was useless at the minutiae of zoology or book keeping. He was the only student not to pass his certificate.

But there was a far deeper, more fundamental problem that diverted him from his studies. Wye College was there to create farmers and John was not a farmer. Until he had set foot on Mr Catt's farm he had never been near one. Not only this, he was discovering that the niche that he was making for himself was not farming first and foremost but people.

He had found his life's work but not really recognised it; the study of people, their relationship with the soil and that through self-sufficiency people can have a great deal of fun living off the land. This had little to do with bookkeeping, and one wonders what he would have done had he actually passed the course. Certainly he was no money grabber and he despised any such activity.

Not to be outdone he tried again to sit another set of exams for a different agricultural qualification. This entailed him working on a farm in the Cotswolds, and sitting the exams in Leeds six months later. He worked really hard at farming, but really poorly at studying. He failed these exams and his self-respect plummeted. His stepfather had already offered him a place in the firm and promised that John could travel to the States to learn more of the business.

John tried life as a junior industrial magnate. It involved him having to be good at what 'Pater' thought was good; playing tennis, cards and going to night clubs. John was bored with it before he knew where he was and he thought the whole idea of this type of business was immoral. He found himself working out the fundamentals of selling oats to millions of people; the costs, the products, the packaging and quickly realised that they were making enormous sums of money. He had, however, omitted the most important point, advertising. Actually making the product was nothing compared to advertising it. Indeed the product itself was nothing; they could be selling soap, furniture or anything. It was the public's response to advertising that counted. John did not like this. He thought it wrong that a commodity that grew naturally in the ground could be advertised and sold at fantastic prices to a supposed gullible audience. He thought it wrong that profit was made for a few from the hard work of the factory workers. More than this it was not John, it didn't excite him or make him tick. He got his mother to tell 'Pater' that he was quitting the family business. Surprisingly, his stepfather was hurt but supportive. He had expected that 'Pater' would wash his hands of him, throw him out of the house and never speak to him again. In the event he offered to pay for John to go back to college, looked for alternative careers and got closer to him than any time in his life. 'Pater' surprised them all since it was he who had point blank refused to pay for either Bill's or John's education.

However John did not return to college but worked on a farm in Essex, making hay and caring for sheep. He thought that he would never really get through bookkeeping.

John did not comment much about this period except to say that it was a great blow to his self-esteem. Looking at it from several decades away it is possible to realise that what John actually did in leaving his stepfather's employment was more than just a brave thing to do. He ran the risk of upsetting his parents and probably there were a lot of unkind words involved on all sides. But what he did was more than a young man just being restless and 'not amounting to much' as Thomas Seymour was fond of saying. It was John taking a moral stance. Whether it was to do with animal welfare, living off the land, the GM debate or human rights, John fundamentally behaved in the same way. He analysed what was going on around him and if he didn't like it he either removed himself from it as quickly as possible, or gave the problem a good hard kicking.

Chapter Two

Africa

Hornsey Island is sinking and in John's day a large amount of the island was already wetland. Before this the Dutch built a sea wall that helped reclaim it from the sea at the same time as they did much to reclaim East Anglia from becoming a briny marsh. The Island's owner, Peg-Leg Stacey, was a rich farmer. He owned Hornsey, some lands to the south and a lot of land in Africa. John, stuck for something to do, travelled the few miles north from Frinton-on-Sea and lodged with Mr and Mrs Burroughs, Peg-Leg's manager. During the summer John cleaned out blowfly struck sheep. Being woolly the sheep get faecal mess around their tails, the perfect environment for blowflies to lay their eggs. The resulting maggots then eat their way through the anus of the sheep causing great pain and frequent death. Peg-Leg, who got his name because he lost a leg in the Great War flying with the Air Corps, had a lot of sheep that were in a bad way and John was busy for a whole summer.

His stay at Hornsey was to change his life. Peg-Leg pestered John with tales of Africa with the aim of getting him to go out there and manage his tobacco plantation. John began to believe there was a life in the dark continent for him, but it would not be in tobacco. He hated smoking with a passion; his mother was a chain smoker and she died of lung cancer. He always hated the 'weed' and never had anything to do with it. Before he wrote *The Complete Book of Self-Sufficiency* there were a couple of similar books on the market that gave instructions for growing and curing tobacco. Neither he nor Sally copied this trend. But John was attracted to the adventure of Africa and he made up his mind to go.

In order to emigrate to South Africa you had to pay fifty pounds to the South African government just in case you left owing money to anyone. And of course the fare for the steam boat had to be found. This meant that he had to explain his plans to his mother, for it was she who would have to come up with the cash. She refused. John persisted and his mother agreed to travel to Peg-Leg's farm to hear all about it. She rather ostentatiously said that she might be persuaded to pay for John's journey if she knew of someone out there who would look after John's moral development. She was given the name of a Farmer Brown in Northern Rhodesia, about whom she made enquiries: she did not get a favourable reply. The company she wrote to about him said that on no account would he be a fit person to care for the moral welfare of anyone. Later John met him. He was dancing naked except for a pair of underpants, playing the penny whistle as Pan would have. Behind him were three naked girls, the oldest of whom was around sixteen.

Perhaps she was right to refuse to put her youngest son into the care of such a man. She did find an association called the '1820 Settlers Memorial Association' to look after John, and with their assurance of care, allowed John his adventure. The '1820 Settlers' were English emigrants who had travelled to the Cape of Good Hope in that year to found the colony at Port Elizabeth. They had developed a network of people whose hope it was to encourage British and other North Europeans to set themselves up in South Africa.

John travelled to Africa on the MV Warwick Castle, among whose passengers was one Sir Ernest Oppenheimer. Sir Ernest was the natural, if not the actual, successor to the British Imperialist

Cecil Rhodes. Between the two of them they controlled nearly all the diamond trade in the world
and a growing amount of gold. Sir Ernest had set
up a cartel that completely controlled the price of
diamonds and was probably the most powerful
man in South Africa. He was interested in politics
and became mayor of Kimberley. He was the first
diamond and gold mine owner to build adequate
housing for his black workers and was known as a
moderniser in his day. He became the chairman of
De Beers and was credited with stabilising the
production of diamonds to match demand during
the Depression.

Sir Ernest Oppenheimer gave the young
'pioneers' on the boat a talk on the way out to
South Africa about how it was the land of opportunity and everyone was goggle-eyed and grateful
that such a powerful man should condescend to
talk to them. A lot of respect was being shown to
him around the ship, but John went one further.
After the talk he marched into Sir Ernest's cabin,
having given his secretaries the slip, and asked for a
job. This show of initiative impressed the great
man and he offered John an interview at his hotel.
John, in a hopelessly romantic way, thought he
would do well working down a mine. The idea of
mine working was planted into his mind when he
was shown down a coal mine during his days at
Wye College. Sir Ernest thought this not good
enough, half promising John a better job. "I'm sure

we can do better than that," he said. He needed
go-getters and John looked like one.

John thought Africa was the most romantic
place on earth. His first view of the continent was
looking through a grubby porthole after having
been woken up by the anchor chain. This spoiled
the experience for him somewhat, and he had to
rush out to the deck to look at Table Mountain in
the early Dawn light. He always regretted his first
view of the mountain he loved so much was such
an unromantic one.

First booking into a small hotel John went to
keep his appointment at the Mount Nelson Hotel
with Sir Ernest. There in the lobby he met a man
who was absolutely mad about mountains and
John, having the happy knack of being able to talk
to anyone straight away as though he was a long
lost friend, was there and then offered a trip up
Table Mountain. John compared his prospects. A
good job with Sir Ernest; no doubt light falling on
him from 'Pater's' eyes for doing so well, no
money worries, importance, big cars. On the
other hand there was the lure of Table Mountain.

With all his riches, power and influence, Sir
Ernest Oppenheimer did not stand a chance. John
chose Table Mountain.

It was to be a pattern of John's life that he
chose the romantic instead of the practical. He
could have delayed his Table Mountain trip by a
few hours, got his good job and then climbed to his

heart's content, but he chose not to. It is almost as though the climb was enhanced by his choice. He *chose* the mountain. To John it was more *real* to turn his back on the *false* world of finance and money and his Table Mountain experience was all the better for it. John would always prefer to be part of something than a paying voyeur, *of* the mountain rather than *on* it, a *traveller* rather than a *tourist*. One can appreciate how infuriating this tendency can be if you didn't understand it, but it pervaded his whole being and determined his attitude to the way he ran his life. It was a major, if little understood, factor in his way with money, his personal time and indeed on his attitude towards women. Later events in his life can be traced to his simple choice of the romantic over what was practical. He made decisions in a spontaneous, almost whimsical, way. The impression this left was of someone who could display great leadership. If someone goes off in a tangential direction, perhaps they know something the rest of us do not? This aspect of his character was always difficult for John to understand since he really had no real desire to be a leader.

Life in South Africa was so different from life in England. To his relief book learning was considered less use than hands-on experience, and since he had been working very hard on farms in England he was well prepared for life at his first stop, the Tarka Training Farm. Here he was better than everyone at the physical work. He found it easy and impressed everyone with his prowess with difficult animals, particularly bulls. The farm was irrigated and fenced out in the centre of a plain called the Great Karoo. The plains were vast and covered with small bushes left there following millennia of climate change. At one time the ecosystem was characterised by tropical rain forest, but as the climate gradually became drier, all that was left were the bushes. These bushes were great for fattening sheep, which was the main agriculture. When the rains came the bushes were carpeted with green grass and when the rains dried up the bare soil returned.

John made such an impression at Tarka that they asked him to stay on as an instructor, but he chose to travel further into Africa as a pupil of a very famous farmer, Oscar Southey. A breeder of Merino sheep, Southey was known to pay huge amounts to import Rams from Australia. The farm was palatial and well built. John's job was to ride around the farm counting sheep in the various quadrants into which the thousands of acres were divided. This allowed him to assess the sheep for fly-strike and to deter the natives from stealing them.

Everyone who was white in Africa called the black people kafirs. The Southeys were regarded as liberal for the time but their treatment of their black workers still upset John. They worked every hour of sunlight and were rewarded with enough maize meal to live off with a few little extras. They had no rights to meat, being given only those animals that dropped dead from natural causes. First though, John had to make sure that the animal had not been helped towards death by human interference. They would cut an animal, or push grass up its nose to hasten death. John proposed that the farm, which had forty thousand Merino sheep, could set aside a few sheep every week for the workers consumption. Oscar Southey poured scorn on this idea with the argument that it would not stop the sheep being stolen.

Native people had no freedom. They were not allowed to leave the farm without a pass and they had no rights to roam within the farm itself either. John likened their life to that of work horses. They were regarded as little more than farm animals that prepared their own food and bedding and produced their own replacements. John realised that the black people were kept as low as it could possibly be for a human to be kept without him or her actually dying. These people were worse off than slaves because they had no cash value. If they died then they died, and were replaced by someone else. It did not cost the master anything. John said they were worse off than real slaves in the West Indies because if they had had a commercial value then they would have been marginally better looked after. John wrote that he did not believe what was being told him that "kafirs needed keeping in their place", that "they would rape your sister", and that if you "give them an inch they would take a mile". He found them to be good people and he was proud to stand shoulder to shoulder with them in the war that followed and they showed themselves in many cases to be better than their white counterparts.

He got to know a bushman named Joseph. The bushmen were described by John as Stone Age people who never worked for white people but wandered around the country living of whatever they could hunt. Joseph had been 'caught' and 'tamed' by the Germans and brought up as a servant.

On one occasion he went out hunting with Joseph, handing him his twelve bore rifle. Once away from the farm, Joseph went to a bush and retrieved a spear, a tool that was illegal for him to own. Lions had been killing donkeys on the farm and they had to be killed before they killed more.

Joseph had a way of tracking animals that was, to John at least, dependent on a kind of sixth sense. He would look at a dislodged stone, a bruised leaf, minute changes in the soil, and would invariably find what he was tracking at a fast walking speed. John and Joseph became close friends. This was borne out by the fact that the bushman took him poaching once, without a gun, when he should have been looking after a flock of sheep.

John could have caused Joseph to be flogged or even put in prison, but Joseph trusted him enough to break the rules with him.

The poaching was for gemsbok, a kind of antelope with huge, rapier-like horns, and they used hunting dogs. When the dogs had cornered the animal, Joseph flashed out with his spear, piercing the animal in the side. The gemsbok would dart out into the bush, to be followed by the dogs and a terrible cycle would begin. Joseph would wound the animal, run and chase again and again until the animal finally succumbed due to loss of blood. Then Joseph opened the dead animal's rumen and both he and John drank the contents. The rumen was the animal's water store, acid and sour to taste but water none the less. John was to comment on this many times in later years. Thus was man adapted to living in all kinds of environments. It was not just Joseph's ability with dog and spear that won him his food, but his knowledge that he could also get water where there was none. Knowledge is an important part of being able to survive, and modern life in cities erodes and devalues that knowledge. As I write in Manchester, a city of a million people, how many of them know how to grow their own food, keep hens for meat and eggs, make cheese and butter, even how to cook properly or make bread?

John found the bushmen to be uniquely intelligent and quick and he met many of them. They lived in small groups, perhaps large families, and they never built anything bigger than a grass covering to sleep in. The leader of the family group was the one to start the fires upon which they would cook their food. Once they killed an animal they ate all of it, save the bones. They would gorge themselves and this would frequently be their downfall. Once full the police found it easier to catch them. They would then be taken to prison just like any other black man at large without a permit, and there they, within a few days, would invariably die, John said from claustrophobia. He also said the Germans were said never to imprison the bushmen, they would just shoot them on the spot. They were treated just like vermin and anyone had the right to kill them.

John continued with the roaming life of sheep farming for a number of years. He was put in charge of a station and eventually got his own sheep. He bought a horse from a mixed race man called Oswald but with it he got himself much more than he had bargained for. Oswald had been a snoek fisherman and tales of blue oceans and cool seas were too much to resist when your daily grind was hotter and dryer than was natural for a man brought up in a temperate climate. John moved to Walvis Bay on the coast.

Walvis is such an important deep sea port that South Africa only handed it over to Namibia in 1994. It has long been the centre of a booming fishing industry. John thought he could get a berth on a boat catching snoek, his romantic mind thinking that he would simply walk into one, but he was very much mistaken. Snoekers were hard men who had taken many years to fight for their places and proven their worth in dreadful conditions working the fish. When John arrived he could not compete and was told that he would never become a snoeker, information that was simply a red rag to a bull in John's mind. He would, regardless of what anyone said, become a snoek fisherman. He was at times very stubborn and if he had made up his mind to do something he generally would. In the interim he went fishing for crayfish on a German motor launch. They caught enough fish and the experience was so exhilarating that he became hopelessly enamoured by the sea. He was determined to become a fisherman. He decided that he needed to buy into a share of the ownership of a fishing operation so he returned to the farm, sold his sheep and pony and, with Clinton, a fellow farmer, he made his way to find a boat. His initial idea was to fish for crayfish, as he had just experienced, but following a long conversation on board the Titania, an American cod schooner, he was to have second thoughts.

Titania's captain, Oscar Johannsen, suggested that John would make a real fortune by fishing for pilchard. There was a heavy stock of these fish just offshore but no pilchard industry in the area. He gave John a lesson in marine biology. Snoek were hunting fish and their prey was mostly pilchard. Now, if the snoek were plentiful, how much more plentiful must pilchard be? Johannsen's idea was to catch pilchard and make kippers out of them. He already had a contact in Cape Town, a Scottish kipperer, who would handle the processing side of the business. Clinton and John raised the money and had a vessel built especially for them in Cape Town. 'The Cunene', named after a South African river, was a forty eight foot boat with a diesel engine. They sent off to Sweden for a ring net to catch pilchard. However, the net was delayed so they left port without it and found themselves fishing for snoek. John had become a snoek fisherman after all.

His crew were difficult; either drunk and hard to find on shore or totally mutinous when the tobacco had run out. But they were good fishermen and great fun once they were under way and sober. They fished for around a year, catching the beautiful snoek, removing their heads which they ate for breakfast, and salting the remainder in big barrels. One time they were fishing with a group of other boats, including the Titania, and found themselves in trouble. During the night the wind changed. Having noticed this John took his boat further out to sea to avoid shipwreck. Titania was not so fortunate and despite the best efforts of Johannsen, she was wrecked on the shore.

Sailing many miles to the south, John's crew spotted two of Titania's life boats. John decided that, because they were in need of cash, he and Clinton would swim out for the boats, sell them in a local port and then return to the ship. They were further, much further away than he had reckoned and swimming out to them was exhausting. They almost drowned. John had given himself up for dead as huge waves crashed over his body, eventually losing consciousness with only his cork life preserver keeping him afloat. It was Clinton who dragged him to a warm piece of sand after they had managed to make landfall. John was completely blue with cold and half dead. They were without water or food and had to walk for two days before they were anywhere near help. Clinton was for giving up and they had to fight with their fists before John could persuade him to continue the journey to safety. When eventually they arrived at civilisation, Clinton was in a bad way, and had to be bed rested. He returned to his farm and John joined The Cunene once again but with hardly enough money to fish. Eventually a company chartered the boat to take fishermen out to sea, and paid John a small fee plus whatever fish he could catch to skipper the ship. This went on for about a year, but John had lost heart. He was to leave the ship at Johannesburg in the hands of the charter company and try his hand at something different; mining.

John was put in charge of forty men in a huge copper mine. He knew nothing of life underground, but the authorities would prefer to put a white man in charge of black men despite lack of knowledge or experience. The working men were itinerants, but the foremen were largely professional miners who lived near the site. They would spend their whole working life down the mine and get to know its geography and processes completely and John, with all his shortcomings, was anxious not to get in their way. John was placed in charge of a sump; a deep reservoir of water that would fill from the liquid falling like rain from above. He had a number of men to help him watch the level and report to him when he had to telephone to get someone to turn the pump on. John stuck at this, and other jobs such as blasting, moving underground trucks and clearing ore, for about six months. He worked slightly differently to other white men in that he would pick up a shovel and physically graft himself, encouraging his team from the front. But maybe it was life underground, or maybe it was the untimely death of a colleague, that caused John one day to hand in his notice. He went to complete a blasting course, and get his certificate, and found himself unemployed.

John heard of a farmer who needed a manager, and so he went for an interview. The man was hugely fat and irksome. He offered the job to John at fifteen pounds a month which he readily accepted. The farm was a mess. Out of a thousand cattle only three hundred remained, most of them stolen and killed by the farm workers. When John told the owner this he simply did not believe him. The owner was too apathetic to leave the house and check his stock himself and had been relying on his foreman who had been lying about the numbers of cattle on the farm. When the farmer countermanded one of John's instructions, he resigned. He had worked there for only three days, but stayed on for a month to collect his money. With his fifteen pounds and a few belongings he wandered north to try for work in another mine. He tried at two with no luck and rested himself in a café where he met 'Spider' Webb.

Spider was a drunk vagrant who wandered from one hostel for distressed British people to another, drinking so heavily that he suffered from hallucinations. "I gets the rats!" he said. He drank his mind into soup. He was married; his wife worked in Johannesburg as a typist but they did not see each other, 'The perfect marriage', he told John. John had no money, but a few possessions, and Spider's plan was to auction them, buy two bicycles and ride south to a small mine where they could get work. So John did just that. He sold his only suit, his gramophone, records and books and raised twenty pounds. Between the both of them they drank the money in the bar that same night.

This was possibly the lowest point of John's

African adventure. He had met with Sir Ernest
Oppenheimer, been offered a lucrative job, owned
sheep, even a part of a sailing boat, worked for
reputable farmers, was loved and happy. Now he
was totally spent, no money, walking south towards the possibility of work in a small mine with
a tramp as a friend and companion.

Together they wandered through the country
and John was impressed at the hospitality of the
people. They were always fed at night in a village.
It was as though the native people made it their
responsibility to be hospitable. Invariably their
meal included a lot of beer, brewed by the villag-
ers. John was to compare this out of hand hospitality to the loss of social responsibility at home. At
one time, he argued, it must have been very similar in Europe, but no longer. Perhaps the invention
of money and credit killed off the principle of hospitality, everyone coming to expect payment for
sharing the basic means of life. John himself was
wildly, perhaps outrageously and extravagantly
hospitable. In later life he simply gave money away
to people but not out of any great personal wealth;
he gave money that really he should have kept to
get himself and his family out of a financial mess.
But then something or someone always came to
bale him out. The principle of hospitality always
has its pay back.

Spider and John parted at Lusaka, John to try
for a job with the Rhodesian Veterinary Service as

a Livestock Officer, Spider to his Rats. He got the job, even though he must have looked a dishevelled mess at the interview. He was given a house, a salary and a vehicle with which to travel around the countryside administering vaccines to cattle. He was welcomed everywhere because the vaccine really worked. There was an epidemic of viral pneumonia amongst the herds and John's job meant that he would walk out into the bush with some servants and a cook and inoculate the natives' cattle. It was an excellent job; enough responsibility to make it interesting, enough freedom to make life worthwhile.

His work took him further into the bush and, together with his increasing number of bearers and helpers, they would walk through areas alive with game animals. John shot buffalo for food. No mean feat since invariably a single bullet would not be enough to kill the animal. According to John a wounded buffalo was the most dangerous animal in Africa. It would turn from a grazer to a hunter and stalk its attacker and even ambush him. John was amazed at the elephants, an animal that John would not hunt because he respected it so much. Many times they were forced to climb trees by great herds of elephants on the rampage. When startled they would cause a great fuss and stampede. John wanted to live there, in the Luangwa Valley, with its heat and mosquitoes and its disease, for ever.

War had broken out in Europe during this time and all at once the world changed. John and his colleagues wanted to sign up for the army but were not allowed to because the work they were doing was of such importance. Shortly, however, with the worsening of the fortunes of the allies, more pressure was put on manpower and eventually John was allowed to join the thousands of other men ready to fight the war against Nazism.

Chapter Three

Far From Paradise

The Enola Gay's war, a B-29 Superfortress bomber, consisted of a round trip of three thousand miles and took twelve hours to complete, an average of two hundred and fifty miles per hour.

John Seymour's war consisted of a round trip of ten thousand miles and took over five years to complete. The Enola Gay dropped one bomb on Hiroshima, killed a hundred thousand civilians and changed the way everyone on the planet thought about their future. John Seymour fired a lot of bullets, killed a few and changed his own life and thinking for ever.

The first weeks of the war was not a good time for the allies; they were being pushed back on

all fronts. The Italians were a strong force in North
East Africa and there seemed to be a mad rush to
get raw recruits from the quiet of South Africa into
the north as quickly as possible. John was part of
that charge. In a convoy of trucks they sped
through the bush ready to take on all comers.
However, when they arrived at their training
camp, a racecourse at Eldoret in Kenya, all the
rushing stopped as the men were camped and then
militarised, that slow, painful process akin to
breaking in a horse. All the marching and saluting
was unpalatable to John. It reminded him of school
days and sapped his confidence. He had joined the
Kenya Regiment of the King's African Rifles and he
was sure that the military life was not really for
him.

His last decade had been spent largely alone.
He had taught himself to think, pretty much educated himself and now he was being asked to behave like a number rather than a human. It did not
go down well with John and John did not go down
well with his superiors. He spent much of his free
time reading rather than cleaning his kit. When, as
a white man, he was brought before the Appoint-
ing Officer to see if he was fit for officer training
he said that his religion was 'Pagan' and his favourite game was Chess. These replies were calculated
to ensure he did not get chosen as an officer and
subsequently he did not have to order anyone
about. Private status would not do for a white man

in a colonial army and so, instead of being bussed off to the Officer Training Unit, he was made a Sergeant.

Two things went right for him in training; he won the shooting competition and he had made efforts to learn Swahili. It seemed natural to John that if his men were speaking that language, he had better get to know it. This got him posted to a Swahili speaking unit, whose members he much preferred to the South African recruits, with their robustly impolite attitude towards black people. The war was something of a poser for John. He did not believe in democracy, thinking there was nothing greater than the individual. He hardly ever voted in elections saying that he "didn't want to encourage them." However, he disliked fascism even more than democracy, and was keen to strike a blow against the iron fist. He always regretted never going to Spain to fight against Franco like so many young men of his generation.

When he finished his training he was anxious to enter into the war. He was put in charge of a platoon of forty men, men whom he respected: John saw the native African as unspoilt by European "grasping ideas about property," and were, in many respects, an intelligent and superior people.

They were posted to Wajir in Kenya, described by John as having a Beau Geste type fort. It was an ancient place, the wells there were said to have been dug by order of the Queen of Sheba.

The fort was heavily defended with concrete pillar boxes, trenches and wires and each platoon was sent for three days to guard it. Most platoons considered it a bind to be sent there but John had an ace up his sleeve. On a period of guard he would slip out beyond the defences and kill an oryx or a gemsbok. His men relished the meat and they ate well. Much to everyone's surprise John proposed to his commanding officer that his unit stay on guard there all the time. Much to John's surprise his proposal was granted.

John and his men ate well and were settled in a place they could easily defend. Disappointingly the expected Italians, with their vastly superior numbers and equipment, never turned up. In actual fact Italians were surrendering all over the continent, frequently without a fight at all. John thought this was because the ordinary soldier did not believe what Mussolini was selling them but later he was to have a more amusing theory about what appeared to be the Italians reticence to fight. Because of this, valuable units were moved to take the fight to a zone where the enemy was showing great bravery, and holding up the progress of the allies.

The city of Gondar was built in the seventeenth century and, until late in the Victorian era, it was the capital of Ethiopia. All around Central North Africa the Italians were giving way to the allies. In truth this was due to their lack of ability in mobile warfare, but General Nasi's soldiers were settled in to well-defended positions. They had held out for nearly nine months and had great prowess in one-to-one combat warfare. They had even taken ground from the allies who were trying to advance. Gondar has been described as the Camelot of Ethiopia, with great castles and mountains all around, the ideal place to make a spirited defence.

John was offered an officership on the way to Gondar, but he refused it as it meant he would have to attend the Officer Cadet Training Unit instead of seeing this romantic city. His refusal was not without some pain on John's part. He felt that he had done well in the army, had managed to walk the line between conventionalism and lawlessness that allowed him the admiration not only of his men but of the officers; John was getting into this war. Instead of more marching and saluting, he embarked on a few weeks mountain training with his men. The assault on Gondar involved climbing high mountains and fighting in steep sided valleys, running up and down huge, rugged mountains in full kit, surviving in difficult and alien terrain, spending freezing nights with no protection and then being taken in trucks, over the high Abyssinian plain, towards Gondar.

The main roads into this highly fortified city were impossible to attack full on, but the British strategists had noticed an ancient track just off the main road which would not have been so well defended. They drove as far as they could down the track and then started to march to predefined sites along the track. Modern warfare demanded passage for huge vehicles, trucks and tanks and so each platoon was given a few hundred yards of track to convert into usable road.

John's willing involvement in the war is clearly demonstrated in one particular episode. During an attack on the Italians, designed to draw them out and work out their strength, John, although not directly involved in the action, volunteered to recover an anti-tank rifle that had been left behind. He "*spent a pleasant and exciting day*" amongst flowers and lovely scenery hunting amongst the enemy for a rifle that was impossible to see in the vast terrain. He described it as being like a picnic. Not so for the man who left the rifle behind who was given a year with hard labour as a punishment.

Gradually they fought their way over plains and hills, nearer to Gondar. Each step had to be won either by hand to hand fighting or by artillery barrage. They usually had one or two casualties each time which mounted up over a period, seriously depleting their numbers. They were pretty grubby and after a few days of fighting they were given time to clean themselves up.

At a fairly secure English camp situated within the field of operations, John's personal servant, a man with the wonderful name of Abdurahaman bin Fadmullah, prepared a bath for him. John was about to step into the bath when suddenly they were attacked by an artillery barrage. His servant nonchalantly sauntered up with some more cold water and during the attack John proceeded to have his bath. Mud was flying everywhere and in the middle of the shelling a friend was hit. So John got out of the bath, put his boots on, (he did not like to walk with bare feet) and strolled over to see how he was - still completely naked. He called a medical orderly who organised the poor man's removal, and John returned, clad only in his boots, to his slightly muddy bath.

The following morning they went into action. They attacked two hills simultaneously and on the top of one John was ordered to take up a defensive position. They watched the battle go on around them and a large number of Italians started to surrender from the airport and a village named Azozo. Suddenly there came a civilian car at high speed containing General Nisi himself, who climbed out and surrendered his sword to John's Lieutenant, a man named Gash. The race was then on to be the first company commander into the city itself. John and his platoon were marched flat out for five miles with Italians surrendering all over the place. About a mile from the city a truck came out and an Italian dismounted, begging them to help save his company from avenging Ethiopians. It was reported in the press that the city was under attack by patriots and that the British had to go in and clear them out. What actually happened was John's unit entered the city and shot at some of the patriots as a warning and from then on the patriots disappeared. John said he did not take part in this shooting. Order was restored in the streets and more British units arrived and they began to sort out the Italians. The Italians had supplies to spare; food, weapons, and lots of ammunition. They had much more than the victorious armies except cigarettes. John thought that after eight months holding out against the allies the Italians were simply gasping for a smoke.

The British had taken eleven thousand five hundred Italian and twelve thousand native troops prisoner. These poor souls were later handed over to Rommel, a master stroke, slowing his forces down and causing him terrible logistic difficulties.

John and his compatriots had been on the march, fighting at times, sleeping at others, for two years. They were expecting a break and some home leave. Of course, John did not have a home to get leave to go to. They had been continually promised that when they had kicked the Italians out of Africa they would be allowed to go home. Instead they found themselves back in Eritrea guarding a huge POW camp and gradually news got through that they were going to a new theatre of operation. At this news one of the battalions went on strike. They marched on to the parade ground and sat down. The result of this action was that they actually won, and the army allowed them their leave. John, with no where else to go, was sent to the Officer Cadet Training Unit, he was after all to become an officer.

For a time John was segregated from others because the army did not want news of the mutiny to get about, but at the Officer Cadet Training Unit John found himself back at school, back to marching, spit and polish and obeying. There was a lot of competition among the cadets but John refused to be a 'blue eyed boy'. But if truth be known he worked just as hard as the rest in polishing his buttons and shining his boots. When it came, being an officer didn't suit John at all. He did not like giving orders as much as he hated receiving them. It was embarrassing to him and this was a feature that marked his future life. He had ideas, but fostering these ideas or even his will on another human was anathema to him.

They were to fight the Japanese and this did bother them. Until now the Japanese were an undefeated army. They had marched their way from their small islands out as far as Burma. The Japanese had a reputation for not valuing life, other people's or their own. If ordered to walk into bullets, they would. The allies wanted to preserve their lives as best they could, and because of this they felt inferior. They trained hard on a slow move north, staying at Mount Kilimanjaro for a couple of weeks and then on to Ceylon.

John loved Ceylon, it was completely different to Africa, a seat of ancient civilisation and spirituality. The food, the people and their philosophy captivated him. Here they were to embark on a year's worth of training in jungle warfare in preparation to tackle the Japanese in Burma.

Officers and men trained together, there was no difference between them, and after three months they marched northwards into thicker jungle. John was sent on a course to develop a guerrilla unit, how to make bridges from bamboo and then blow them up and how to disarm booby traps and mines. The idea was that if the Japanese invaded Ceylon the guerrilla units would be left behind to disrupt their progress while everyone else evacuated. John called his a comic opera unit, and they were supposed to be the toughest men in the company. They marched into the jungle for weeks on end and blew things up. They killed a lot of fish with explosives, upon which they depended for food. Then after some months the units were disbanded, probably because the threat from the enemy was not so imminent.

It was in Ceylon that John came to know the peasant way of life, and he loved it. Above all the Sinhalise peasants loved to work and they were always singing about it. Most of the work was related to religious ceremonies. John thought this was exactly how things must have been in the

West generations before. Feast days were linked, especially obvious ones like harvest, to the work on the land. In the middle ages a man had to pay a day's work for his home and land to the manor, and the rest of his time was his own to devote to growing food and being happy. There were sixty feast days which were holy days; compare this to modern living!

It was here in Ceylon that John formulated his ideas about native people having an ancient, more true, way of life. He felt that the peasantry might have been living this way for millennia, so quite possibly all those years ago everyone lived in the same manner. In studying native people the world over, now, in the twenty-first century, you could be looking at how Europeans might have lived millennia ago. Somehow, civilisations diverge, introduce technologies, compete with one another and either die away or succeed. This point of view is not exactly logical, but you can see where he is coming from; it does show that there are ways of living that are generally easily sustainable over very long periods. As a theory it does not take into account the effect of the development of even simple cultures and neither does it account for the effect of one culture on another. He was to use this thinking as the basis for *Far from Paradise*, a television series and subsequent book, co-written with Herbert Giradet.

Whenever he got leave he would get a travel

warrant to some hill station where, instead of 'hobnobbing' with some of the English middle classes, he would get off the train and jump on a bus to some remote village or other. It was possibly in one of these backwaters, stagnant backwaters as it turned out, that John contracted amoebic dysentery and had to be hospitalised. It really took it out of him, not least because he was living with the disease for a month before it was diagnosed. After a month in recovery he was fit to catch up with his battalion who were now well into the Burmese jungle in pursuit of the Japanese.

Burma was a morass of death. Remnants of a Japanese army; dead men, skeletons being picked at by animals and flies, lay all along the roadside. Burned out houses with charred bodies inside them became temporary shelters for the African troops and their equipment. Finally, when John caught up with his men at the battalion camp, he set up his bed. Ten minutes later he was on patrol with his platoon and his bed, along with a fellow officer who was sitting on it, were blown up by a mortar. The terrain was difficult for fighting and the Japanese were capable and worthy adversaries, but the first enemy John met was already defeated.

The Japanese were at the extreme of what their supply lines could cope with and they were starving to death. They had been marching from Japan and many considered their officers and rulers had simply let them down. He saw two men sitting by a hut who appeared to be dead, but their eyes followed him, moving as he passed by. They were so weak that they were unable to brush away the maggots that were eating their faces. John could do nothing for them, and his superior officer killed them as a humane gesture. Years later, when addressing the inevitable fate of a lame horse, John pointed out that if it had the choice, would it choose to be put down - which was the inevitable fate of many a sick horse in this country. One wonders if his mind went back to this tragic and, for John, heart breaking moment. It also told him something about the character of the officer who did the job. He was unwilling to order someone else to kill the men, he did it himself. Was his action of kindness in killing them considered a gift? Was there a moment of communication?

This was a sad army. They had roared across the continent, each man strong with a month's rations. Three months later they were decimated human skeletons, a disgrace to humanity in that they had won nothing but death. John compared it to Napoleon's retreat from Moscow; but this was far worse. The only way to deal with the death was to burn the bodies with flame throwers, a horrid job which would have destroyed the best, or worst, of men.

John crossed a river with his men and a captured a Japanese soldier. They were so proud of him that they gave him food, tea and cigarettes. He was scared to death because he had never seen a black man before and thought they were cannibals and would eat him. At this time John and his men were the furthest east of the whole 14th army. Here, deep in the jungle, John met James Thurber, author of *The Secret Life of Walter Mitty*. John was given one of his books and was 'shaking with laughter' at what he read.

As they moved east, the Japanese were fighting fit. From here the war was dangerous, and a number of John's men were killed. Ngombe was a scout on such a fateful day, he was also, in John's words, "no more than a kid". His job was to creep forward looking for Japanese, and it was very difficult work. It is a slow, careful job but Ngombe was terribly slow, so much so that John called him back for a telling off and told him that he thought he was a coward. So off Ngombe trekked again only to get himself shot by a machine gun. He fell to the ground screaming. With bullets cracking all around John crawled to him. His hand was almost severed at the wrist and he was hit in the stomach. As he lay dying he was heard crying for his mother. The rest of the assault was slow. Climbing, throwing themselves on the floor whenever machine guns were fired and keeping a look out for bunkers which could only be attacked by artillery was a slow and bloody business. Ngombe's death had upset John. He genuinely loved these people. He had already refused a 'pip', an extra badge on his lapel making him a captain because it would have meant that he would have been second in command of the whole battalion and consequently loose contact with his men.

The cycle of attack was repeated for weeks. Slow forward movements with the foremost scout being killed, then a nest of around half a dozen Japanese being blown up. Where there were larger concentrations of enemy the artillery was called in, raining down hundreds of shells in a small area, ripping the countryside to pieces, causing devastation everywhere. Japanese soldiers did not like this at all and who could blame them? One time they ambushed a large number of enemy and captured an ammunition dump, but usually there was little contact with them, they simply melted away. It was a long and very nervous walk.

At Christmas they were all transported by air back to Assam for a rest and John was sent on a course to use the new British three inch mortar. He was promoted at the same time and returned to his unit as a captain. He trained his men in the use of the weapon and while returning from a training mission he experienced two things. Firstly the sound of the cuckoo, with which he had no recollection for at least a dozen years, and secondly the news of the attack on both Hiroshima and Nagasaki. The Enola Gay and The Great Artiste had done their job. All their wars were over.

At first John felt frustration. Not being able

to tackle the enemy and all landings in Malaya had been cancelled. The war had not so much petered out as prematurely halted. It was as though someone had thrown a full stop mid sentence. Later John was to think more deeply about what had happened. He was angry with the Americans to do such a thing in the first place. To kill two hundred thousand people at a stroke, many of them civilians who had no chance of finding cover, with such a terrible weapon was a cowardly thing to do. He thought it typical of someone who sat behind a desk somewhere. He was later to say that he was ashamed of being on the side of a government that could do such a thing.

He was demobbed back home where he spent his time walking around East Anglia forgetting how to be a soldier. He had the time and the opportunity to wander around the countryside and become English again. He bought himself a double decker bus in which he lived and found a job with the Ministry of Agriculture. The government needed to do something humane with the hundreds of thousands of POW's in Britain. They could not be sent home, back to a country totally devastated by war. The Ministries of War and of Agriculture set a department called WarAg to channel some of them into agriculture. John was in charge of finding and co-ordinating the work of prisoners of war on the land in East Anglia. It entailed visiting farmers and arranging for POWs to work on for them.

During the time John was away in Africa and at war farming had changed in the United Kingdom. Farmers were now office men arranging deals on the telephone. Small farmers were going to the wall, their land being bought up and used to make large farms even larger. The fields were becoming bigger and hedges were removed to facilitate larger and larger machines. More importantly, the people that once lived on the farms, labourers and farm workers, were vanishing. A combine could do the work of hundreds of men, and these people were being forced into factory life, council housed and protected from the so called harshness of their former lives. Economics and accountants had moulded life in the fields into an inhuman place, driven over by tractors but rarely trodden by feet.

Consequently the once vibrant communities surrounding the farms and villages, were becoming barren and empty. This was a change that John resented. When the ordinary folk left the land there was no one else to keep up their traditions and their way of life. Changing the demographics in the countryside had a knock-on effect; blacksmiths, thatchers and any number of important skilled workers disappeared from the end of the forties onwards. The attitude of the land owners towards groups of people like gypsies was not the same as the attitude of the ordinary country folk who largely saw them as someone to be welcomed. Over a decade or so the countryside, in John's mind, died. At best it was very sick and John was to set about recording what was left of it before it went altogether.

Above all, he spent his time in pubs, or sailing, and in his flamboyant way telling stories about his time in Africa and his journeys with the army. He had a lot to relate and was an excellent story teller. Someone suggested that he should write his tales down and send them to the BBC. He did and they were accepted by editors who were clamouring for interesting, outward looking material about foreign parts, about the war and how England was changing.

John's life was about to change for ever.

Chapter Four
People and Places

The few years between the end of the war and his marrying Sally Medworth were spent on the move. As the WarAg department began to run down its operations, John was in the market for new direction and he started to work for a programme on the Home Service called Country Magazine. In East Anglia he found a never ending source of people to interview, telling of their ordinary, frequently vanishing way of life; almost always a romantic existence to soothe the ears of post-war Britain. He became quite a regular. His stories were in the aural tradition that was seen to be so important at the time. There was a recognition that the world was changing and that a lot of lives led in a traditional manner were just disappearing. John interviewed people by the score, wrote scripts and used his own life experiences to entertain and inform the great British public.

Out of this came not only radio programmes, but books based on the people he had met. Someone came up with the idea of a journey across land to India, where he could record the way people had changed in Europe and the Sub-Continent after the great events of the middle of the century. He also did a separate tour of India and shortly after this he married Sally. India herself had only recently become independent, and the culture of the ordinary Indian held a fascination for the ordinary Brit in a way that it never had before her independence. In a way it might have been a forerunner to Michael Palin's *Around the World in Eighty Days*. I dare say it would have been a whole lot easier to go around the world by surface transport in the late forties than it was a generation later, so much for air travel. The BBC paid him a hundred and seventy pounds to make his way over land and sea and record whoever he met along the way.

John was not formulating a great model for living at this time. That was to come later. He was simply enjoying himself, indulging in the company of interesting people. He was to paint a picture of people who were self-reliant, or alternatively of people who were spongers in the age old tradition of oppressing the poor or swindling the government. It is possible to read the accounts of those he met on his journeys either around Europe, India or around Britain, on her water ways and rivers and see how the people he met influenced the philosophy of living in later life. Since his snoek fishing days John had cultivated a love for the sea and boats, and it was only a matter of time before he would engage in a great journey around the coastline of England and the English inland waterways, but marriage and a child would come before this.

His journey from London to Greece, via France, Switzerland, Austria, Yugoslavia and Bulgaria highlighted the difficulties that countries had following the war, but it was Yugoslavia where John found contrasts among the people worth reporting. There was little in the way of food, yet the people seemed to be reasonably well fed. He was impressed that they had managed to avoid mass starvation despite the war. The whole land had been fought over time and again and the infrastructure was destroyed. Bridges were blown up, ships lay sunken in the Danube, roads and railways were no more, and there were few public buildings. All the people were working very hard at building, repairing and agriculture. They were committed to the idea that if they worked hard now there would be a reward later. They seemed to like General Tito and there was an atmosphere of progress.

Holdings greater than thirty hectares were nationalised, but the majority of the land remained in the hands of the peasantry. They were encouraged to link up their farms to form collectives, but this was a painful process. Field sizes were small and inefficient in terms of mechanisation. It had taken the UK two hundred years of starvation, political unrest and misery to change the economy from agricultural to urban. Yugoslavia was trying to achieve the same in only five years.

John did find people in Yugoslavia prepared to talk about politics, both for Communism and against it. He had supposed that it might have been a country where there was a lot of martial music, where everything was either black or white and that there were to be only official points of view. He did not find the people so indoctrinated and was amazed to hear them talking freely about what was wrong as well as what was right. The people had given mental ascent to what Tito was doing, and were prepared to argue about it as well. On the whole he found that communism made no real difference to conversation. People talked about football, work, food, women and families in just the same way they did in England.

There were new factories. John saw a tractor factory and the young people went about taking on jobs in organisations such as making a park out of a bombed urban wilderness. One thing he did find in abundance was generosity. Train guards made a great party of the journey and bought beer and wine by the jug full at every stop, not allowing John to pay for his share. This was more true in the poorer Bulgaria where food was handed around, black bread, cheese, boiled eggs and raw onion.

Bulgaria was even more a peasant based society than Yugoslavia and it was clear they struggled to look like a grown up country because of it. Soldiers searched the train and, not for the first time, officials believed John to be a spy. There was evidence of a lot more indoctrination but people were still people. The guards behaved badly towards John because they did not want to put a foot wrong or be responsible for messing up. John realised they were uneducated people being forced to do a job for which they were under qualified. These people, forced into uniforms, were really peasants, farmers and fishermen. They had great skill at farming and fishing, but not at soldiering or secret policing.

If only Bulgaria had remained agricultural instead of chasing the spiritus mundi of the modern world as seen in the late 1940s. One wonders what John would have made of it as a modern agricultural state. John described her as 'old fashioned' and a long way behind the twentieth century. Irrigated farming was beginning to replace dry agriculture in the fields, which looked primitive.

There were a large number of Turkish people who had avoided the rigours of the modern Ottoman Empire and still more the changes of Kemal Ataturk, still wore traditional dress and lived a traditional life in the fields. Horse powered water pumps matched horse powered road transport and the crops in the fields looked to be of low quality. The infra-structure that matched this peasant way of life must have been equally primitive and, to coin a former idiom - sustainable. What would we give now for such a nation that does not pollute, that feeds itself, has its own deep seated culture and traditions? The mad rush towards western lifestyles has consigned such nations to European history.

Kemal Ataturk was famous for forming the new state of Turkey out of the old Ottoman Empire. He is widely quoted and considered wise. 'Nationhood belongs to the people' was the cornerstone of the new state, formed in 1923. The whole nation would be based on a broadly republican ideology and as the first independent Moslem country, a totally secular society was planned. Christians, Moslems and Jewish communities thrived together without any appreciable tension. "We are a nation without classes or special privileges" he said, and this was certainly true when John appeared after some twenty five years of nationhood. The first president, Kemal Ataturk also stressed the paramount importance of the peasants, who had long been neglected in the Ottoman times: " The true owner and master of Turkey is the peasant who is the real producer."

John did not seem to have studied Ataturk that much. He commented on the socialist nature of Kemal Ataturk's policies, not because he was interested in communism but because, like the Eastern European states around them, there were not that many capitalists to build a new industry base for them. What John did see was a mix of old and new. Trams being pulled by horses being dodged by large American cars. He saw good education, a reasonably well off poor and a large number of fat rich people, healthy children and good schools. The Turkish were forbidden by their founder president to wear anything but western dress and they seemed to do well on it.

Looking at the photographs of John's time in Baghdad you could be mistaken for thinking they were taken yesterday. The people look remarkably familiar. They seemed to have had attitudes that are also familiar to those you hear of today. John was regaled with stories of how Iraq could have taken Israel easily if they hadn't been ordered not to by the Americans. All the nations of the Levant, Syria, Lebanon, Iraq and Jordan should join together and be strong. This concept was proposed by a middle aged bank manager from Mosul, and the whole of his carriage were ebullient about how

they could take the Jewish homeland if they
wanted too. They were equally antagonistic about
America because of their support for the new
state. How many times has this story been repeated?

As the train wandered towards Mosul, a man
tried to bribe a customs official. His luggage was
full of jewellery, watches, gold and other commodities. The bribe was not accepted and he was
led away, moaning and crying about his fate and
trying to argue that they were gifts for his family.
The bank manager, the same bank manager who
suggested the merger of nations, had no sympathy
for him. His lack of compassionate zeal was nothing to do with the sanctity of business, but with the
method by which the desperate man tried to bring
goods into the country. There were, apparently,
tried and trusted ways of smuggling goods into
Iraq. Camel trains were the best method, or else
he should have offered the official a decent enough
bribe.

The penal system in Iraq was seen by John to
have an unusual way of administering justice. People remained in prison until they had paid a suffi-
cient bribe which was commensurate with the
crime committed. Young men brawling in the
street had a bribe to pay much the same as young
Englishmen would be bound over and pay a fine to
the magistrate. The former paid money to men
who would use it directly in the local economy,

the latter would pay money directly to the government. As a system, John noted, it worked. How fairly the system worked was a different matter.

Persia, John found, was a land of corruption, poverty and confusion. There had been so many attempts to get it on its feet, and they were currently led by an American 'seven year plan.' This was farcical in that no one was ever willing to do anything except in self interest. They saw public office as a way of gaining from bribery, and did not understand the western way at all. A friend in Tehran suggested to John that India had benefited from British rule and was a hundred years ahead of Iran, so Iran should have been governed from London, at least for a while. The Shah had built dozens of palaces which remained empty and cost a fortune. All around was poverty and despair; a lasting image was left in John's mind of a family settling down for the night. The husband kissed the wife and both kissed their child, over whom they wept. The were to sleep on the pavement, huddled up against the walls of one of the Shah's palaces. Poverty and riches, an old story.

The corruption and the poverty of the nation had an affect on the people of the country, often because those within in it wanted to change it for the better. Such was the case of one charismatic Imam who raised revenue to build a hospital for the poor by begging on the streets dressed in rags and bullying government officials. Work on the building was all but complete with just one wing to finish when work stopped as the necessary girders were delayed in port, held up by customs. John reported that the Imam was cross about this. "If a businessman wanted a radio for his mistress he could always bribe one through customs, but girders for hospitals could not be done." Another story was that the Imam had been visited by the Shah who had been told that if he wanted lunch he would have to eat the same food as everyone else, bread and mast, a kind of curdled milk. This was laughed off by the Shah, and he did arrive to visit the hospital. When he found out that there was actually nothing to eat except bread and mast, he stormed off in a temper.

John and a 'hanger on' named Mohesh got themselves into quite a bit of trouble when on a journey to swim in the Caspian sea. They were arrested by police who thought them to be spies, a recurrent feature when Middle Eastern met West in the shape of John Seymour. Mohesh proceeded to argue with the captain of the police, saying they were both important people and anyone who messed with them would be in trouble themselves. The policeman was sure they were spies, and so he 'imprisoned' them in the hotel where they drank vodka and played backgammon with the proprietor to see who would pay. However, the content of John's notebook was to make life more difficult for them. He had a writer friend, Bertie Chapman, who occasionally wrote scripts for 'Dick Barton Special Agent,' the popular radio programme. John had scribbled a picture for Bertie of a Whaler in his notebook in preparation for a script and this image eventually found itself before the Persian army authorities. It looked like a warship and to the Major, who was questioning them, it was complete evidence that they were spies.

In a master stroke, Mohesh told the Major that they actually *were* spies. They were on a mission to find who among the people would be sympathetic to the British, who would be trustworthy to receive support - financial support. The Major was completely taken in by this and began to ingratiate himself to them saying that he loved them so much that it must have come from God. He would gladly give his life for them, an offer that John thanked him for. A telegram had come from the British Consul, directed not to the army, who were holding them, but to the police. The Captain of the police wanted a bribe to pass the information on to the army, and when none was coming he denied all knowledge of the telegram, so John and Mohesh thumped a few tables and made a fuss. Eventually the Army Major lent them the money to travel with some prisoners to Tehran, where they found their freedom. I don't suppose the Major ever got his patronage.

Leaving Persia for India, John travelled through the sub-continent at the time of partition and creation of the state of Pakistan. He collected many dreadful stories of popular uprisings and massacres perpetrated by Hindus against Moslems and vice-versa. Trainloads of people were killed, or thrown out of the top floors of buildings, and the mass movement of races led John to sympathise with everyone. The authorities seemed to simply stand by and watch, and the country was in a mess. Pakistan was merely a year old when John passed through and people were healing their wounds, physically, spiritually and morally.

After a five year absence John flew to his spiritual home of Ceylon. He described an elephant kraal. The land owner made a huge fence out of tree trunks buried into the earth, and tame elephants were used to capture and 'break' the wild animals for use on farms and in general work. One bull had to be shot, an unheard of experience. He was simply too violent defending his cows and human life was in danger. The shooting affected everyone, and John, who had climbed trees to avoid elephants in Africa, had a long held affection for these huge animals.

His journeys to India and Africa continued over a number of years. He was to make many friends and fill many tapes and notebooks for the BBC and the subsequent books. There have been many travelogues produced for generations, even millennia past but John was possibly the first to concentrate almost exclusively on the ordinary people he met on his way.

Now, this little book is not about all the places that John visited, or all the journeys he undertook and so I, quite unashamedly, am missing out much of his travels abroad. The reader is directed to John's books which beautifully paint pictures of worlds past. In particular, *Sailing through England* is as gentle as the scenery it depicts, a beautiful read. I would like to paraphrase a passage from this book which describes John's way with the people he met.

He had skilfully navigated past the Boston Grand Sluice in *Jenny the Third*, which is a considerable obstacle between the tidal Witham and the city. John was allowed by the lock keeper to tie up by his narrow-boat and Sally, Jane and he went to walk into the town. Soon, by a beautiful row of fishermen's cottages that are still there, painted in pastel colours along the riverbank, they came across a piebald pony in which Jane was rather interested. The owner was a talkative man, small, almost small enough to have been a jockey. This was the key to his opening up to them; he had been groom to Lord Mountbatten's polo ponies, was a jockey in Egypt, and huntsman to the Nizam of Hyderabad. These days he travelled the country around Boston with his pony and cart delivering furniture and the like. He had just sold a cart to some gypsies. No ordinary gypsies mind; one of them was said to be the King of the Gypsies.

John's ears pricked and no sooner had he worked out where they were he slung his tape recorder over his shoulder and tracked them down. He was at first assailed by their dogs, huge lurchers that ran from the gaily painted horse drawn carriages. Within a few seconds some middle-aged people came out to greet him, asking what he had under his arm. They already knew, "Give us five pounds and Len will tell you his life story, he's the King of the Gypsies!" John's reply did not please them and they began to be antagonistic. "I'd rather throw my money over a bar!" Everyone knew they were not going to get money out of him.

John sat on the floor and said that they were mad to be travelling around the country on roads. What they really needed was a boat with which they could move freely around, live comfortably and not be bothered by the police. On land they were only allowed to stay for a day to rest their horses, and then were moved on. He told them about *Jenny the Third* and one of their number called him a water gypsy. At this they calmed, and William Lee did indeed tell John his story. He said he was born in Cardiff (he had a Welsh accent) and he had travelled all around the country. He was seventy-four years of age, but felt as though he was sixteen and looking for a new wife. The current Mrs Lee gave him a poke in the ribs.

All the young men were out in the pub and the girls were out selling, but times were hard for them. They had no rest from the police, something they blamed on travellers, not gypsies. They said that not everyone who lived like them were gypsies. They strongly disliked people who pretended to be gypsies, and called them 'half-bred mumpers'. There were some who looted and robbed and the blame went on everyone. Gypsies would never rob anyone they pressed. They knew what the tape was for; someone had been doing much the same and the tape was broadcast on the radio. A woman called Mary grabbed the microphone, "This is Mary so and so speaking. If my husband, William, hears this will he come back to me and my baby, because I am waiting for him. It is time he came back to me."

William Lee made money by selling horses, but the times were hard, and John wondered if he would exchange his horse drawn caravans for motor ones. "I wouldn't have one if it was given me!" He was emphatic, he had lived all his life in the same way, was perfectly fit and never had had a day's illness. Theirs was a healthy life, one which they were born to: A life of horses, dogs, fairs, travelling, people, pubs, singing and story-telling, everything that comes their way. John walked back to Boston, through the suburbs, and thought them dull.

Chapter Five

The Broom Years

John's book *The Fat of the Land* is probably the most well known after the self-sufficiency guides of the 1970s, and it is totally intimate; a picture of a growing family in a wilderness that was to be slowly tamed. For many, myself included, this book was inspiring, and pointed a way to a life that could only be dreamed of. By the last pages the dream appeared to be slightly more achievable than when the book first called to me from a dusty shelf in an even dustier old bookshop. It was read from cover to cover, and when the last page was turned I started again at the beginning. It was my was my evening companion and my early morning call.

When John left WarAg, it was to write scripts, record country folk, edit the recordings into features for radio programmes such as *Country Magazine* and to write books. He lived on his old bus much of the time, which was ideal for his purpose. A couple of trips abroad and a couple of books left him reasonably replete financially and he bought a boat, *Jenny the Third*. She was a Dutch barge, flat bottomed, comfortable and easy to sail. In 1954 he married Sally Medworth, an event we shall read of later, and together with Jane, their first born, they set about exploring first of all the inland waterways of England and thence both the coasts of the North Sea, the English side and the European side.

The nomadic life, sailing around inshore Europe, was not ever going to be safe enough for a family, and as Jane grew into a toddler, it was time that John and Sally found a house to live in. *Jenny the Third* would have been adequate for John, and I dare say Sally too, but slopping around the North Sea with an infant in such a boat was becoming increasingly hair raising. Although Sally had been born in England, she knew very little of it so it was left to John to find them somewhere to live. East Anglia was a trendy part of the UK at the time. People with money enough to escape from London found themselves populating the long bulbous

coastline north of the Thames. Besides, John knew
East Anglia. He spoke their language, the rural dis-
tricts of Suffolk and Norfolk were his first port of
call when looking for a place to call their own.

This decision to become land lubbers was
taken on tour. They found themselves, not for the
first time, afloat in darkest Yorkshire. The Leeds
and Liverpool navigation is today quite a cosmo-
politan affair. There are smart 'rural style' houses
in new stone to match the Yorkshire standard
creamy yellow buildings and along the 'cut', as we
say in these parts, there is a feeling of prosperity as
the motorway and the motorcar has made it possible for people to live in rural towns and villages
and work in cities like Leeds or Manchester. Back
in the 1950s it was a very different affair. Soot and
smoke changes the colour of Yorkshire stone from
light cream to a depressingly dirty brown. The canal in those days was beginning to stop up in places
and parts of the stretch from Leeds to the centre of
the Pennines were at best described as dismal. A
popular song sang in Oldham, Lancashire ends
with *"Now we're touching Yorkshire's line. I can't see
owt passed there but grime!"*

A Pennine winter in the mildest of years is
not a pleasant experience but the winter of 1956
was particularly bad. Indeed, the weather for the
whole year was abysmal. The worst rainfall since
records began was in August of that year when a
whisker under eight inches ruined everyone's holi-

day. Everything froze in January, thawed and froze again in February.

They had, for reasons lost in the mists of time, moored her for the winter at a part of the canal called the summit, but the Leeds-Liverpool canal was no place for a vessel that had such a pedigree. They had managed to rent a stone cottage from a farmer and *Jenny the Third* was moored alongside. They woke one morning to find Jenny submerged in six feet of freezing, dirty water. John must have kicked himself since the sinking was largely his fault. He had forgotten to turn the sea cock on the lavatory system off, the water in the pipes to the toilet had frozen and in the thaw the pressure had broken the pipe and flooded the boat. John had long been confused about the plumbing on board Jenny. There were pipes everywhere, not all of them obvious what they did. He paid out good money for a plumber to try and sort them out, but he failed. After the sinking it seemed that everything was ruined, belongings awash, books soaked but worse of all was the effect of freezing water in the engine, which had cracked because of the expanding ice. *Jenny the Third* was eventually unceremoniously towed to Hainsworth's Boatyard in Bradford for repair. John described this as a sorry place for a sea going vessel to be stuck.

However, the temporary loss of Jenny brought a marked impetus to their house hunt, though the actual process seemed to be a little chaotic. John thought the sale of the repaired boat might bring enough to cover their debts and at the same time provide them with a deposit on a property. It was not to be. The winter came and went and they had to leave their cottage and they ended up in a wing of an old Tudor farmhouse, lent to them by a friend.

In terms of the actual type of house they had in mind, they seemed to have specific needs that had to be fulfilled; room for Sally's pottery, John's writing, children, drunken friends, maybe a horse. Having looked at more than fifty properties they decided they would buy a field and build their own house from the timbers of old boats. John found such a field in Holbrook overlooking the Stour. They would manage, somehow with Jane toddling about, to knock up a building, filling the spaces between the timbers with wattle and daub in the old fashioned way. Not having any experience in building did not deter them at all, but dreams are not always solutions, and they did not buy the field. Perhaps John's enthusiasm for the project struck a chord in the seller's mind for some years later there was a house, just as John had planned, but built from brick by a qualified builder.

They had quite wisely written to the owners of country estates with the object of buying or renting a suitable property. There was a large decrease in the numbers of people living in rural

areas with the consequence that lots of properties
were literally falling apart without inhabitants.
One reply, from Michael Watson, offered them
the chance of a look at two cottages belonging to
his farm which he didn't want to fall down but they
were very remote

John and Sally went to view the property
which was in Orford, in Suffolk. Orford had been
a village from before the twelfth century, when the
castle and the church were built by Henry II who
also created the safe port. Henry stayed at the castle from time to time, a structure that cost around
fifteen hundred pounds, around a tenth of the an-
nual Royal income. Ten percent of the current
royal income is a huge amount, and emphasised the
importance Orford had in those early days.

It took ages to trundle up the farm track to
reveal a forest plantation, a double thatched cottage and a marsh. Miles from anywhere, its re-
moteness was made up for by the rent, which was
at first offered at only ten pounds per year. John
actually paid twenty five pounds plus rates for the
double house and five acres which became known
to thousands of avid readers as 'Broom'.

John's twenty five quid a year translates to
current costs of around a hundred and sixty
pounds per month. It was stipulated in the tenancy
agreement that they would keep the property in
good repair. This fell short of the modern
'repairing lease', where hapless tenants agree to

spend so many thousand pounds on their properties in order to bring them up to modern standards at their own cost while paying a reduced rent. A modern day repairing lease costs in excess of five hundred pounds each month as well as the cost of upgrading the property. When the lease comes to an end the rent is then hyped up in line with what is called current commercial rates. Clearly landowners have learned a lot over the years.

It seems strange that as John needed to earn a living by writing for the BBC he should go and live miles from anywhere. It caused problems which dictated the way that life at the Broom was to progress. They bought a Bedford Dormobile to move furniture, work on the farm and for John to travel around the country. He had just finished a programme for BBC radio called *'The Voyages of Jenny The Third'* and was about to embark on more.

John's favourite pub was 'The Ship' at Blaxhall. It was well known for its large tap room and the congregations of ordinary folk who loved to sing. Here John met singers like Harry Cox, Geoff Ling and Cyril Poacher, and a whole gaggle of people interested in collecting the oral record of ordinary working men and women. In 1956, George Ewart Evans was working in Blaxhall on his classic book *Ask the Fellows Who Cut the Hay*. How much John was influenced by Evans' seminal work is not really known. It seems to have been extremely popular at the time. People were seeing their ordinary way of life change and were desperate to record it before common every day things disappeared altogether. In the true spirit of the time, John embarked on journeys to record the history of country folk for the BBC. Some of these recordings remain, and some of the material has been written into books, but on the whole a lot of this work is not available. There were many countryside projects John covered. In many ways his recordings and conversations were the basis for his later work, he was to rely on them as basic research material.

Programmes such as *The Secret People, a picture of Romany life*, were typical of his work. It documented life as it was in the days when gypsies were allowed to stay where they wanted, and as it had become in the late 1950s when they were harried from one place to another by police or farmers. It gave details of their work and daily life, looked into the problems of educating their children and expressed their sense of inferiority because of their illiteracy. Yet most of them would not trade in their nomadic life.

He was also to work on *The Severn Speaks*, a series that investigated the lives of the people who lived along the banks of the river Severn, from its source at Mount Plynlimmon in Montgomeryshire. Among them he interviewed Richard Davies, aged 94, who was bewildered that no peaceful use had been found for nuclear science. Mr Davies spoke movingly of the purpose of man. In Llanidloes he interviewed factory workers who cultivated their own smallholdings as a link with their agricultural past. In Berriew, Montgomeryshire, Maldwyn Thomas, a schoolmaster, spoke to John about his attitude to fishing as a sport which "fulfils one of man's deepest instincts." Amusingly, in Newtown, described by John as the 'Leeds of Wales,' a male speaker denounced the flimsiness of the then present day male underwear and saw it as a symbol of decaying virility. This tour continued through Welshpool and on to Shrewsbury to speak to coracle men. He recorded stories of Roman ghosts in Wroxter and interviewed interesting folk in all the river towns as far south as Bridgnorth.

The Age on the Wing was a series of six programmes of 'living memory' about the former life of the English countryside. These six programmes of memories of village life sixty years prior to the late 1950s, *"before the motorcar and the builder had swallowed up the distance between town and country"* were recorded by John in villages of the Midlands and East Anglia, from Shropshire to Suffolk. John wrote in the Radio Times,

"When the people of that old generation have gone they will be gone for ever. It will never again be possible to make a series of six radio programmes like 'The Age on the Wing'. We shall no longer have the live and lively words of old men and women to speak to us. In making this series, I spent many months meeting several

*hundred old people, and recording all those with what is
loosely called "broadcasting voices". It is usual for old
people to idealise their youth, but even allowing for this,
I was driven to the conclusion that in spite of the ine-
qualities of income, the poverty, and the hard work, the
"good old days" in the countryside were actually very
good indeed."*

John's final radio programme in the
'Broom' years was for the regular BBC production,
'Counterpoint'. In 'A Time of Poaching' John interviewed a number of poachers and gamekeepers
about their trade, how to despatch animals, avoid
detection and the relationship between the poacher
and the gamekeeper.

Of course, all this recording, as well as his
other writing was time consuming and made life
pretty difficult. He was away quite a lot, a recurrent problem that was at this time a necessary evil.
Sally, throwing herself into the home with remark-
able energy, joined him in decorating the house,
but continued at a greater pace when he was away.
Everything was hard work, a toil, a culture shock.
Getting to know the water pump, the building,
starting to clear the garden and grow some vegetables, moving furniture, painting the walls, knocking through the two houses, all of these things
were new experiences. John was forty three, Sally
was twenty four and they moved around like "ants
whose nest had been turned up with a spade." Neither of them were prepared for the encounter, it

was desperate hard work.

Friends arrived at various intervals and "paid for a moment of enthusiasm", as John put it, by knocking through walls, or building pump houses or fencing or decorating. John admitted to finding domestic work boring, but he liked the results of Sally's handy work. It was Sally who made a home out of the two houses, stripped the walls, filled them, redecorated. It was John who cleared the walls out, rebuilt them, sorted out buildings and all the structural work. And then there was the roof.

Thatched roofs, more or less, last a generation depending on what kind of straw they are made from. The ridge of the roof at the Broom was made from wheat straw which only lasts a decade. Thatching straw, frequently called Norfolk Reed, grew in the local marshes and would last much longer because of the inbuilt waterproofing protecting the plant from the damp environment in which it lived. The Broom badly needed rethatching on the ridge and the back side, where it came down to near the ground level. John bought a load of Norfolk Reed for seventy five pounds. An old friend from John's London days, Jeremy Burnett along with his wife, and Alan Waller, a folk violinist, thatched one side of the roof and gave it a new top.

Alan remembers the time well. " I was taking time off from being an industrial chemist with my folk violin at the time, and met John in a pub in Orford where I was playing a kind of folk music pub crawl. My motorbike broke down, and John volunteered to take me from pub to pub in his car. He asked me to play in the car while he was driving which I did, when all of a sudden I was aware of the most magnificent drumming. It was John playing on the roof with both hands and driving with his knees." Their tour of the pubs in the area took a long time and they returned home early the next morning.

Suffolk at the end of the decade following the Second World War was alive with artists. Benjamin Britten premiered his children's opera 'Noye's Fludde' at Orford Church in 1956, and lived in the area. Alan Waller remembers that John was not a part of that set. He was present when Alan was playing in a malting hall in Aldeburgh and listening in one corner was Britten and Gustav Holst's wife along with the famous singer Peter Piers. They were checking the acoustics before buying the building for the now famous Aldeburgh festival.

As was usual in the Seymour household, if you stayed you got to help out, and Alan found himself being invited back for Christmas. Apart from helping out with the garden, the farm and the house, Alan was pleasantly locked into a lifetime friendship with John and Sally. In those days at the Broom, John and Sally were a team. They had their differences and this showed in their daily lives then and later, but they converged and met in a single point; they both had a great capacity for love.

In all of their dealings with people they retained a compassion for people, an easy empathy which simply made people happy. This was a trait they passed on to their children. For John, life at the Broom was not about self-sufficiency, it was about loving; loving Sally and the children, loving what he was doing, loving the landscape and the way of life he was beginning to make for himself.

But life did begin to wear them down. If on Monday you walk a round trip of three miles to get your milk, it might be an adventure. If, three weeks later you are still having to walk that far each day for milk I bet it would be just about driving you mad! It certainly did John. He *"slogged over the warren with empty milk bottles and slogged back with full ones."* He was starting to think of a cow. He was also thinking of a petrol driven pump for water and a pump house to put it in, a study and a pottery for Sally, a dairy and a wash house. Life at the Broom pinched a bit just because it was so hard. To collect enough water to wash the nappies took a long time, let alone all the other reasons for having water. So they started to direct their energies into making life more convenient. Some of the modifications were simple, others were life changing. Brownie, their first cow, was such a change.

"Brownie was brown - darkish brown, too dark for a Jersey, skinny and bony, and swag-bellied...a sweet silly frightened old thing." Why a cow? Well the trip to the milkman for one thing. They were offered, but didn't buy, a pedigree Jersey for a hundred and twenty pounds. As John said, *"... you can buy a lot of milk for a hundred and twenty quid!"* A cow on the premises brought a number of problems, none the least that she needed milking and since John had not milked a cow for over thirty years, it took a while for the technique to come back. But it did come back, and John has since taught hundreds how to do the pleasant morning and evening chore.

Brownie gave four gallons of milk a day so a dairy and the tools needed to process all the excess milk was needed. John, Sally, Jane and newly born Anne simply could not drink four pints of milk each day but they could eat butter and cream and cheese to their heart's content. Consequently they needed creaming bowls, cheese presses, sieves, churns, scotch hands and a clean place to make butter, milk, cheese and yoghurt. But even the greatest gluttony could not consume everything that could be created from four gallons of milk a day, so they ended up with pigs to finish the milk off.

Alan Waller remembers life at the Broom as "great fun." He described John as "simply magical" and you could forgive him for anything. John

had a way with people that was based on personal
generosity. Not the kind of ingratiating generosity
that expected something in return, neither was it a
generosity that was simply there to get people to
like him. John was not a weak man, he was able to
stand up to bullies and he was not averse to a bit of
rough and tumble if it was necessary. But John was
such a man that he gave of himself, his money and
time and quite naturally received in return. Alan
Waller was a little surprised when John took him
to Richard Pinney's oysterage and stole a dozen
oysters, eating them there and then. He took the
shells inside Richard's house, where a goose was
being roasted on an open fire. Alan did not realise
the oysters had been paid for, not in money but in
friendship.

Richard Pinney and John were contemporaries. They thought alike. Richard lived in London until the end of the Second World War. Totally fed up with the city and the dangers of the
war, he decided to move into the countryside. A
long search found a derelict old cottage where he
started making and selling rush mats from the
natural resources around him. From this start he
turned his attention to the oysters that had been
fished in Orford for centuries. Locals warned him
that he would be throwing his money away, but
like John, he took no notice. The native oyster had
been in decline for some time, possibly because of
the changing nature of the water. Orford is on the

estuary of the River Alde which rises near Fram-
lingham and flows to Aldeburgh. Here it is de-
flected by a long shingle split that now extends ten
kilometres and is growing by fifteen metres a year.
Richard Pinney was described by someone who
worked for him at the time as a man who was loud
in a merry sort of way, and who loved to drink.
His wife was said to have been the major industri-
alist in the family. Richard realised that although
the local oysters were having a hard time, the conditions were perfect for the Portuguese oyster,
which he imported. He was right and the new
stock thrived.

Alan Waller suffered a bad fall from John's
horse, Pinto. John got him home where he and
Sally plonked Alan on the kitchen table and rubbed
him all over with whiskey. Alan's relationship with
Pinto was frequently comical. The horse never
liked pulling the plough and one particular day,
when John wanted to use the 'Jalo' - a kind of
horse drawn hoe, the animal refused point blank to
co-operate. The Jalo was used but not in the way
that is described in the *Fat of the Land* for it was not
Pinto that pulled it along but Alan Waller.

Pinto was a plucky chap and he was a big
part of the Seymour family. John describes a journey to the Ship Inn in the governess cart. The old
men of the pub welcomed him as though he was
royalty and insisted that he allow them to put
Pinto back into harness when it was time to go

home, well after midnight. John was always gleaning information from the old chaps who lived in the villages and farms around the Broom. He was never short of advice, indeed he was famous for buying something at a farm sale, not really knowing what it was used for and searching out the appropriate old chap to tell him what to do with it. This earned him a reputation that was not really justified. Many people came to think of him as someone who made things up as he went along, not a real farmer at all. John didn't care to tell them of his farming apprenticeship, his time at agricultural college, running many a farm in Africa. He had experience in farming beyond that of many of his neighbours. What he did not know about was a world of farming that had already been lost. Only the machinery of that era was left and there were still many who just about remembered how to use it.

The first horse John had at the Broom was called Fanny. She was a heavy Dales pony, and was quite lame. She had ring-bone and had to be sent back. The replacement, who was Pinto, arrived with some great difficulty, from Yorkshire. A friend's son, George and his wife, had brought the animal, but had trouble with the horse box and the wheel had fallen off seven miles outside King's Lynn. It was late at night. The young couple walked the horse into King's Lynn calling at every house they passed for help. They received none until by chance they met a man described by John as a "rough old potato merchant." They had walked for hours and had now reached King's Lynn centre. The old chap stabled the horse and found them a bed at a friends home and lent them his own horse box the following day to finish the job. On top of this kindness, he refused any kind of payment.

John's choice of words in the narrative of this story in *The Fat of the Land* is important. He called the people who refused to help 'gentlemen farmers' and the person who did help a 'rough old potato merchant'. He also used the words *noblesse oblige* to describe the due behaviour expected from the noble, in this case the rough old chap. The rough old man cared about the young couple's plight, the gentlemen farmers didn't. The inference was that the older people lived by a different set of rules. It's as though John predicted the differing treatments from the two groups. He wouldn't even have expected the 'gentlemen farmers' to give a second thought for the plight of a young couple but knew that the 'rough old potato merchant' would.

In order to make the countryside work you have to love it *and* its people. You cannot have one without the other because if you don't care for the people around you it is symptomatic of a greater selfishness. A selfishness that will lead you to mistreat the land you farm and the world you live in.

As Oliver Goldsmith put it, you cannot have a
happy people living off the land if its owners love
their money more than their soil.

> *Ill fares the land,*
> *to hastening ills a prey,*
> *When wealth accumulates*
> *and men decay.*

Wealth has accumulated in this corner of
East Anglia. Farms have merged, become bigger
and people have become smaller. The current
landlord of John's favourite pub, The Ship, says
that it is was now dead. The pub is dead, the village is dead. It is populated by second home owners who work away. He has a lot to say about people who glamourize the past as if they really were
'good old days'. He thinks the poverty, the exploitation, the sheer hard work was not worth going
back to. But John would have said to this landlord,
whose pub is now shut and for sale, that he missed
the point. At least there were people living there
in the old days, a vibrant community who grew
their own food, caught their own fish, married
their own women and depended on no one else.
The village now is populated by people who de-
pend on the far side of the world and its international trade for their food, who exploit whole continents for their livelihood and in doing so destroy
the very ecosystem that keeps us all alive.

Broom's five acres were not really enough for them to expand their operation into full self-sufficiency. They could not grow cereal crops because they needed the land for grass and there was not much more land available for them to rent. They had to move and it was Sally who wanted to own the land she lived on. Why they should up sticks and move to Pembrokeshire, the other side of the country, is not documented. What is known is that the children stayed at a farm in Pembrokeshire while John and Sally looked for a place which they eventually found at the foot of a mountain.

Chapter Six
The Mountain of Angels

Fachongle Isaf is hard to find. It is also very Welsh. When John and Sally moved there in 1964 they were treated to the traditional welcome of the Welsh: silence. People on holiday in Wales often think the locals rude because they do not gush out with sentiment and overt welcome, but within a short time the true warmth of the Welsh comes out. "Are you the Englishman?" said George Hughes, a "square, aquiline, rather handsome old man," when John was fixing some old barbed wire along the road. Contact had been made and from then on John and Sally were treated with friendly respect by their neighbours.

As I said, Fachongle Isaf is hard to find. On the hottest May day for many a year we were travelling to stay with Anne, John's daughter, and her husband David through high hedged welsh fields on single tracked roads. "No, this is wrong. We've gone too far!" The colander of roads in the Pembrokeshire countryside all looked the same and we were lost. Years before Lindsey Hutchinson, Vicky Moller's first husband, was travelling to see her, now John's third wife, and he could not find the place either. He stopped on his BSA Thunderbolt motorcycle and asked a chap who was mending the road if he knew the way. "Oh, you mean the loonies!" By this time in 1978, John was a well known character in Pembrokeshire. But Lindsey did not have the same insight that we had provided by John's descriptions of the countryside he had come to love.

The mountain, John's mountain even though he never actually owned it, had been the home of a number of different peoples over the millennia. John describes the life of Saint Brynach who lived on the top of the mountain. Legend had it that Saint Brynach was fed by angels and that the mountain had become known as the Mountain of Angels, Carn Ingli. This mountain had been farmed for over two thousand five hundred years and the remains of large settlements were obvious all along the ridge peak. Although it had never actually been

John's mountain, spiritually it was where his heart was.

Looking about, driving nearer to Haverford West than we should have done, we saw a mountain with all 'wobbly' bits of black rock on the top of it and knew instinctively that this should have been visible from John's farm as he described in the book *Blessed Isle, One Man's Ireland*. So we circled around the base of the mountain and drew up directly to the farm, hidden deep in trees and green countryside. Back in 1966, John and Sally's first view was not quite so arboreal. Far from being a land of "gloomy mountains and wet sheep," they found South Wales to be a wonderfully open country, fertile and, above all, not a pheasant in sight. John didn't like pheasants. Dare say he liked to eat them, but they represented to him a misuse of the countryside. Acres and acres of land set aside to keeping these cosseted animals hidden from predators and unavailable even to the men who had to look after them, but shot in their hundreds by bankers and landowners. Wales, at least this part of Wales, did not have much of a history of pheasant shoots. It was a "country that belonged to the countryman!" By which he meant that it was the peasant that *owned* the country. They being proud people would not have liked to be described as peasants.

Not everything from the Broom actually made it to Wales. They sold the pigs for a start.

They also handed over the cow to their landlord
Michael, whose son remembered the special fla-
vour of her rich milk some forty years later. The
rest of the menagerie was carted in a huge cattle
truck over three journeys in the middle of the
night. They journeyed at this time not only to
avoid the traffic but because the vehicle was so
large that it only just fitted down the narrow lanes
and this leviathan wouldn't allow other road users
to pass and keep their own lives in the process.
There is nothing to indicate whether John even had
the correct licence for such a vehicle. He simply
referred to it as the whale, and out of it's belly
came all they owned in terms of furniture, livestock and equipment.

The farm, when they arrived, was a complete mess, much worse than the Broom had ever
been. Nothing was fenced, the building was unin-
habitable and had been used by their neighbour's
stock for a long time. They had to chase off a number of animals from the land, both sheep and cattle, and they had to build secure pens for their
own. They lost a horse and found it again five
miles away. Then John started work on the house,
cleaning it, glazing it and making it inhabitable.
There was plenty of water, but only one tap, so
John learned plumbing, at great personal cost because the hardware shop was miles away. Frequently he got home to find the thing he *really*
needed was not in his grasp, and so he would have

to trek back and forth. And then there were the floors and the doors and the windows and the internal walls and the fires and a million and one jobs to be tackled. It was two months before they were able to stop cooking out doors on an open fire and move the Aga into its correct position, smashing the old Rayburn to pieces and selling it for scrap.

They arrived at Fachongle Isaf, the name of the new farm which translated means small low corner, in late spring. A wet, warm spring means that grass grows quickly, and in Wales it grows faster than in most places. Being extremely busy with the fabric of the house, their first crop of hay was cut and bailed by a contractor, and hundreds of bales had to be brought in for storage. Sally and John had what they referred to as the 'fish van', which was a small ford van. It carried only a dozen bales at a time, but they were hard at it loading them into the small vehicle, transporting them to the stack yard and starting all over again. They were both surprised by two tractors pulling trailers carrying Welshmen; a dozen or more drunk, singing Welshmen. They collected the bales and helped stack them, and then continued to consume around ten pints each of strong home brew. They had met their neighbours.

The neighbours were singers, community people with a strong sense of belonging. Although fiercely competitive, from the best of flowers to the best of beers, everything had its meaning and importance in the light of whether it was better than someone else's in the formality of the local competition. There were country fairs, beer competitions, singing competitions and, of course, rugby. Not that we ever hear that John played that immortal game. Welsh society formalised the competitive side of their lives, thus setting free the rest for community affairs. So it was normal that the men should come and help the Englishman with his hay because the hay needed collecting and stacking. It would be a shame on them if John's hay had rotted in the field, and more than this it was a signal to John and his family that his faith in taking on such a property was to be applauded. Incidentally much the same happened to John a dozen or more years later when, as an Englishman in Ireland, they harvested his crop for him, not out of a sense of community like the Welsh, but out of a sense of love for the individual.

Fencing was a job that needed to be done around the whole farm and it was seriously hard work. The soil in Suffolk came from the sea and was fine, well behaved soil. The soil in Pembrokeshire came from a retreating glacier some ten thousand years ago and was full of erratics. An erratic is a lump of rock floating in the glacier which fell when the ice melted. Rock of all sizes, from huge boulders to pebbles, were dropped all over the county and this made sinking posts for fencing a totally frustrating job. In order to make fields easier to plough it was necessary to dynamite the larger rocks. Dynamiting happened to be John's largest contribution to the economy of the district. He was the only one who was trained to use explosives and had the certificates to prove it, and he was in great demand for the job. It entailed going to the police for a permit, to the quarry to buy the explosives and then to the field to do the job.

Much of the land in Pembrokeshire is steep, and soil was periodically washed away in the constantly falling heavy rain. Their pigs chopped up the steeply sloped land and it simply flowed away in torrents. It became necessary to terrace the land to keep it still.

They bought calves from markets and raised them, frequently via terrible illnesses. and sold them as cattle or placed them in their milking herd. John did not like this work. It was illegal to sell calves younger than a week old but some dairy farmers saw this ruling as an uneconomical waste of time and would sell the calf as soon as possible, usually younger than a day or two. These calves frequently became sick because they lacked the benefit of the colostrum in their mother's milk which was available for only the first week of life. John and Sally worked hard to keep them alive. At least the calves John bought did not suffer the fate of many, simply shot and left to float down the river to the sea, as one farmer in Yorkshire described to me as all too common a practise.

John and Sally were drawn into commercialisation of their farm by necessity. Now I can feel some readers will have their hackles up at that word commercial. Which of us can live in this country without paying their way? Self-sufficiency is really dependent on 'rendering unto Caesar' that which (as John would put it) the 'Thing' demanded. The 'Thing' was what Cobbett described as the machinery of government, the tyranny of finances and banks and the valuing of human life and endeavour in terms of monetary value. In the end you and I work, everyone works in one form or another in order to pay their debts and in pursuit of this John and Sally flew headlong into commercial farming. They joined the Small Farm Scheme, which meant they had to improve their land, increase their stock and work in a manner dictated by the then Ministry of Agriculture. John found the system worked in a way many a farmer sees it working today. Schemes and subsidies trickled money into farm businesses. Rather than accepting dribs and drabs of charity in order to dance to the government's tune, John found himself wishing they would simply give him a decent return for what he actually produced.

It wasn't the stocking, or improving of fertility that caused problems. It was the draining that nearly broke them. They engaged a contractor to drain the central marshes, two sodden fields of four acres each. Starting in winter (the wrong time to attempt such work) meant that it consequently took a long time and was very costly. They had to find a thousand pounds to pay for this, money that they simply didn't have and the world seemed to be pushing them in a direction in which they didn't wish to go. The result was personal frustration on a grand scale.

John started working again for the BBC, and was away from home a lot. Really, from the early 1970s, John was to embark on a frenzy of writing in order to make money to pay for the farm in one form or another. Sally took on the work on the farm often single handed, which was, in a way, what she had been doing for many years. John's long periods working away made this an important necessity. His friends, with the kindest of intentions, said that John was very good at thinking and at writing, but Sally was the one who did all the work. She was largely in charge of the farm while John was interviewing and writing. It has to be admitted that for John there were many temptations and these temptations were frequently too much for him. There had been other women and Sally had for a long time felt neglected as well as taking on all the work alone for much of the time. Life was not quite as comfortable for either John or Sally as he portrayed in his books.

Glasnant Morris had built his own home further along the valley from John and he was asked to give Sally a helping hand with jobs she could not

manage herself. Sally enjoyed his company and after a while an affair between Glas (as he became
known) and Sally had sprung up. John returned to
make it clear in no uncertain terms that his rival
was not welcome (with the aid of a shotgun), and
that he wanted things to be right between himself
and Sally. They tried through a difficult period to
patch things up but strained relationships are often
not easy to repair under the pressure of work and
finances and the team that was John and Sally
broke up.

John wrote about the episode in *I'm a
Stranger Here Myself*. He did not write about the
actual break up - just his feelings of the time. He
had gone to collect *Willy-nilly*, his twenty foot
coble boat, open to the elements and used for fishing in Northumberland. It was powered by oar and
sail and John had to scrape her, paint her and sail
her back to Wales, from Orford down the
Thames, up the Oxford canal and into the Severn.
From there round the foot of Wales and by St
David's Bay into Pembrokeshire.

He saw Broom, now much changed and being kept as a holiday cottage. It had been considerably cleaned up, John would say sanitised. The
out-buildings of the Broom had been pulled down
and the fields had been turned in to immaculate
lawn with no food produced there at all. John
stayed in the cottage while he set Willy-nilly ready
for the journey and as you would expect, the

memories flooded back. He slept and woke with
ghosts. Perhaps for the first time in his life he felt
lonely, not merely alone but truly lonely.

It was the source of a great deal of regret for
everyone, not least for John who entered a period
of his life that was feverishly productive and not a
little chaotic. Wherever they went, people loved
him, they simply couldn't help it. It was something
in his character that, as Alan Waller pointed out,
"You just had to love him, no matter what was going on." The only time Alan was ever cross with
John was on May 30th 1971. He wrote it in his
diary. John turned up with a new bride. Frances
Hurdle was the wife of an art lecturer in Bristol,
Victor Hurdle. He and John were great friends,
and the circumstances surrounding John's courting
and marriage to Frances are a little unsure, but
Victor was certainly a willing participator in the
proceedings. John and Frances arrived at a folk festival at which Alan Waller was playing. John described them both as "love's young dream", and
Alan was annoyed because he thought a great deal
of Sally. John didn't mind though. "That's all
right!" he said to Alan, and it was. That was
enough to placate his wrath.

John's marriage to Frances Hurdle did not go
well. It was turbulent at times, expensive most
times and certainly a strain on both of them. They
lived for a period at least in the caravan between
the barn and the house. They spent time apart as

Frances went back to Bristol and then John would go and fetch her and they would try again. It ended in some unpleasantness.

The move to Fachongle Isaf coincided with John becoming more involved with ecological movements. He, along with Leopold Kohr, Fritz Shumacher and Ivan Illich, started the magazine *Resurgence* with John Papworth. The latter became famous as the 'the shoplifting vicar,' a name applied to him as he controversially did preach in his church that, if you had no money and you were hungry, it was not a sin to shoplift from supermarkets. This was not a statement about the human condition alone but a dig at the supermarket culture which had, in his opinion, placed nearly all of the food sold in the United Kingdom into the hands of just four companies and that these companies made small farming very difficult, if not impossible.

John Papworth was a great and close friend to the Seymours. His affection for them was reciprocated, and they remember still his ability to be sitting at the kitchen one minute and reciting acres of Shakespeare the next. John Seymour respected his intellectual prowess and he learned a lot about concise writing from him. Some time later Satish Kumar replaced John Papworth at the helm of the magazine and took it in a more Buddhist, more self-enlightenment and spiritual direction which John Papworth didn't like. The founding editor thought himself 'pushed out'. Papworth founded another magazine, *Fourth World Review*.

Satish Kumar believes strongly that he was being true to the small is beautiful message, particularly its political aspect. And that this message needed to be presented in the context of spiritual, artistic and aesthetic values. Without these values even small can be ugly. Satish commented that "John Papworth and I disagreed on this, he thought that I was diluting the message and making the magazine of general interest."

The twenty fifth anniversary of *Resurgence* saw a meeting at which John Seymour was to be the main speaker, but Rev. John had not even been invited. John Papworth remembers with great warmth John's actions. Not only did he refuse to be a speaker unless John Papworth was invited, but when he did speak he said, "I cannot possibly address a meeting such as this without first bringing John Papworth to the stage."

Out of necessity John wrote for anyone who would pay him but much of his writing on ecological matters was voluntary. He became involved with a number of major thinkers and organisations of the time; the Schumacher Institute, patron of Green Books, friends with the family of Lady Eve Balfour of the Soil Association and the Centre for Alternative Technology, He wrote eighteen books during this period, some of them guide books to various places or coastlines. Then in 1976 he

wrote the *Complete Book of Self-Sufficiency*, followed
in quick succession by a couple of seminal works.
Bring Me My Bow and *The Countryside Explained,* both
published in 1977, spoke of John's philosophy on
the countryside. One commentator said that *Bring
Me My Bow* was John at his "outspoken best". It was
about England and John's hopes for an England
with a low sustainable population. He argued for
the splitting up of the United Kingdom and for a
political system based on small units. It was really
an anti-globalisation treatise before books on this
subject became popular.

The *Complete Book of Self-Sufficiency* was John
and Sally's best seller. It helped establish the publishers Dorling Kindersley as a major producer of
information books. In it John explains the nitty-
gritty of living off the land. Much of it was John's
thinking and Sally's experience. Needless to say it
brought a lot of money into the farm and made
them a household name. A consequence was an
upsurge in interest in the other books, and John
ended up writing a sequel to *The Fat of the Land*
called *I'm a Stranger Here Myself.*

With these publications John became the
leading light in the self-sufficiency movement. He
had dealings with a number of groups in the
United States, mostly Farmsteaders (their equiva-
lent of Smallholders), and one particular idea from
the US caught his imagination. It started with the
purchase of a shed, a big shed, more of an army

hut, that he really didn't have a use for. He bought it cheap; his family said he always bought things cheap that he didn't really need. John takes up the story himself:

"This old army hut shall be a Centre!" I said. "And I shall call it Canalfan Fyw, the Centre of Living. A movement shall start here that will radiate out over the countryside, and bring people back to the land, and fill empty cottages, and rebuild the ruins, and the singing of men and women and the laughing of children shall once again ring through these woods and these fields shall become fruitful again!"

Jane married, Sally remained on the farm, and John came in one day to say that he had placed advertisements in various newspapers for students to join his self-sufficiency course. There had been little in the way of consultation over the project. Sally was part owner of Fachongle Isaf and it became necessary to buy her out. Sally moved on, some miles away and Dai and Kate went with her and Anne went to college; John was alone.

One of the respondents to the advertisements for the 'Centre for Living' was a young Londoner who was looking for something in life. Vicky Moller described herself as someone who was looking to live off the land but felt somehow unable to do so. She wrote to John asking to be considered for a place on the course.

Her meeting with John was quite dramatic, as he described to Anne. "She took all her clothes off and jumped in the estuary!" This action had a great impact on him. She was energetic and vibrant and within a very short time they were talking of marriage. Vicky was, and still is, totally in love with John. We all discussed this time. My wife, Diana, Sally, Vicky Moller, Anne and her husband David and myself, sat around for an evening meal in the house in which John died. Vicky looked Sally in the eye and they both smiled.

"Of course, I went to Sally to ask her permission if I could be with John." said Vicky. It was a touching moment, one of warmth. Here were three women who totally loved John still. Sally had said that Vicky should be with him because he needed someone to look after him.

'The Centre for Living' became chaotic. People arrived, some stayed, others left and the whole affair was terribly expensive. John was spending all his time writing in the 'penthouse' which was basically a small room at the top of the house. They had little control of what was happening on the farm which began to resemble a commune of disreputable types. People from all over the world arrived ato the Centre for Living and John became less able to look after them. Vicky described him as "incontinent with regard to money", which at times he seemed to simply give away. One evening John had recently been paid for some writing, the proceeds of which he simply gave away to the course members and long term lodgers. Vicky was livid with him.

Vicky and John had a son, Kett, a practical person who had inherited John's affinity for the land and still lives on the farm he was born into. His new family, which included Vicky's other children, were the 'excuse' to disband the Centre for Living and get the farm cleaned up. This was a mammoth task and took some time. It was at this time that John had been up the mountain, not only to commune with the angels, but to look in another direction, westwards.

Vicky had not noticed John's yearnings for a change in direction. Angela Ashe had come to the farm when she was fourteen for a holiday, and simply didn't leave. She was described as very beautiful by Anne and Vicky. John and Angela struck up a unique relationship and John later described her as 'being like another of my daughters' and Will Sutherland, later to be Angela Ashe's husband and Johns co-author, described them as being like brother and sister.

John had massive debts, despite a large income from his books, television and radio work. In the book *Blessed Isle*, John infers that he left his farm to his children when he finally moved to Ireland. In actual fact this was not true. A consortium of family members divided the farm between themselves and paid John the full market value of each share. In this way he was bailed out of financial trouble and at the same time the farm remained in the family. Vicky Moller, living in the farmhouse of Fachongle Isaf, was completely surprised to find John going to Ireland with Angela. She spent years hating and loving John for what he did until the pain subsided and only loving him remained.

In many respects John was uneasy about this period in his life. He had, in a way, experienced personal failure, and shadows of it were seen in his writing. Describing Saint Brynach as being fed by angels in the *Blessed Isle*, he commented that angels never fed him, "but then I (he) am not a saint!"

Chapter Seven
The Blessed Isle

The move to Ireland was a time full of contrasts. One wonders if the line "I have loved both well and dangerously," in his poem Envoi refers to this period of his life. John and Angela had a unique relationship and, bearing in mind their age difference, sharing the same house didn't have the effect one might expect on the locals. They warmed to John immediately. After the confusion of the Centre for Life it has to be said that Angela provided for John a secure base from which to settle into his work in a more organised way. John said himself that he was very untidy and she tidied up his life as well as his desk. He had been to Ireland many times, either working for the BBC or simply as a visitor. He loved the people who seemed to be a mixture of his singing, step dancing friends at the Ship Inn at Blaxhall and his Gypsy friends from around the country. He found them to be culturally strong, having their own outlook on life based on deep traditions and a harsh history. Above all, it was a flamboyant, party island where John fitted in wonderfully. They had a terrible history of cruel dealings with the English; one would almost expect the place to be melancholic, but it was quite the reverse. Perhaps the more you oppress a people the more reasons they have to find for being joyful.

John and Angela moved in to what he described as a "run down" cottage owned by a friend, Jim Wharram, at New Ross, County Wexford. Jim had previously lived there with five women, but it all went sour for him when a man turned up and took one or two of them away. Back in Pembrokeshire, Fachongle Isaf had split up. John was financially a little stronger, although he hardly ever had much money, and the first thing he did was to make the building habitable and the land productive. Simultaneously he found time to take to his heart the history and the culture of the Irish people. His first trip to Ireland had made him many friends; making friends was a knack for which he had a great capacity.

John had been advised to move to Ireland by his accountant who had a mistaken view of the Irish Law which said that income from artistic endeavour is not subject to income tax. Eventually John found out to his cost that the accountant was wrong, because it was only works of fiction that were tax exempt, and information books were just as taxable as they are in the UK. According to James Wharram John appeared one day and said "I need somewhere in Ireland!" and James had just the place.

James and John had been sailing friends; James a designer of catamaran sailing boats, John an avid and experienced seaman. John had wanted one of James' boats for a long time. James was also a serious drinker and, like John, he enjoyed a good time. They all travelled to Ireland to look at the house, James and a female companion, John and Angela, returning on the night ferry. At the time the Irish ferries were quite rough affairs and James settled down to sleep on the floor. Around one o'clock in the morning he remembers John appeared kicking him in the ribs to wake him up. "Get up and dance you bugger!" There was a room full of Irish folk singing and dancing and John did not want his friend to miss out.

John agreed to rent Kilowen Cottage (later he bought it) returning to Wales only to retrieve a few tools, some books and clothes. John seemed to be starting afresh; a new life with Angela. He had left behind the accumulation of thirty years. With only a few tools and a rotavator they set up home. Kilowen Cottage had an acre of fenced garden attached to it and two acres of rough pasture on the other side of the lane, running along the River Barrow.

The cottage also had a boat which would get some sterling service. The river is tidal as far back as the town of New Ross and this allowed them to row upstream with the tide, do their shopping and then row back with the ebb a couple of hours later. The cottage had its own little stone-built quay to land on. They eventually bought a traditional river craft, a *prong*, which was around sixteen feet long and had a sloping front and a flat bottom. This was ideal for their purpose, as estuaries mean mud and a prong will toboggan along mud flats.

When it came to working the land John met with much the same response as he had in Wales. However, this time there was more of a social class slant to the help that his neighbours offered him. Farmers in Ireland had always been poor, desperately poor, something that John attributed to the fact that the Landlords, who were basically the English invaders, had exacted huge sums for rent for every parcel of land. But since independence the ordinary farmer owned his own land, and with the advent of the EEC, later the EU, lots of money was pouring into Ireland. Farmers drove big cars, had huge combines and the latest tractors. They drank the best whiskey and were generally very prosperous.

As John was about to till the land with his baby rotavator the people objected, offering him help with a multi-gang plough pulled by a tractor. Then, as John was about to broadcast his seed by hand on the field they once again objected. It simply wasn't done like that any more and they offered instead to drill his field in a few minutes with the latest seed drill. John harvested the wheat with a scythe and stacked it in the traditional way with Angela's help. It was the final straw and the neighbours distracted him with drink while they stole the whole crop and fed it through the combine to thresh it for him. It was more than a neighbourly act, it was a statement. People in Ireland didn't go around threshing wheat over the back of a chair anymore like poor people did. What might have been accepted as quaint in Wales or England was simply socially unacceptable in Ireland. They were better off than that!

Straight away John found that the rapport that had to be dug deep for in England, existed on the surface in his new home. People wanted to be friends, and those he knew a dozen or more years ago on his first solo trip not only remembered him but picked up the relationship as though they had never been apart. John had met Paddy Burke that first time round and the minute he walked up to him in Duncannon Fort, Paddy remembered him (and of course they ended up in the pub). This was no ordinary pub, for inside there was a group of musicians. There was also a set of Northumbrian pipes, a violin and a small drum called the Bodhran, an instrument said to be at its best when made from the skin of a greyhound. There was a whistle, dancers and a whole list of singers - everyone in the bar actually. People of all ages continued to arrive and when the bar was suitably full out came the violin, and everything else and the reels, jigs and hornpipes began. The music was Irish, but not the Irish music you would hear in Dublin in just the same way that what you would hear as folk music in many pubs in the 1950s in England was not like 'official' folk music heard on the radio.

Every nation seems to be able to provide evidence of their population being full of bards and lyrical poets. It is sad that the Americanisation of England has largely done away with such raw entertainment. As you travel west through Wales where the national sport is not rugby but poetry, and into Ireland where the pubs today are still famous for their music and song, there seems to be an increasingly tangible free sprit present when it comes to ordinary people. There you will find people who are not really looking for a career in singing or playing, but just love traditional music and play, sing and dance in pubs and homes and halls just for the fun of it.

John and Angela loved these gatherings. They would travel miles to various pubs, some of them literally the size of a small room in a house or a converted half of a shop. Eventually John and his friends organised themselves into what he called Raiding Parties. A group of people from a pub would land in another one in in a different area and take it over. They would dance and sing and share their music. They became very popular, and they travelled further abroad holding raiding parties in Wales and also in Austria. John received a coveted silver medal from the Austrian government for his work in ecology and culture, and also the keys to the city of Salzburg, taking a raiding party with him, having a wonderful time almost putting the ceremony into the shade. John had formed a friendship with Leopold Kohr, the Austrian economist and the first to coin the phrase 'Small is beautiful'. They were contemporaries in the thought, the very logic, that underpinned the green movement, but Leopold attacked questions such as 'why are we miserable' from an academic point of view, where John thought he already knew the answer to such queries. To John all of the foundation of human happiness was based on the deep seated urge and need for human beings to be closely associated with the land that they come from, not the country but the very earth itself beneath their feet. Every form of human joy in one way or another swelled from this single point of view:

"Give a man an acre of land and he will provide healthy and happy families, contented with life and a credit to their race."

John and his raucous music and dancing was the antithesis of this academia and highlighted culture as the moulder of societies more than words written on a page.

Many years later John was on tour selling his books to bookshops from a van. He was in the Province of Northern Ireland and being naturally thirsty found himself a pub. The pub was decorated on the outside with a huge Irish tricolour, and it was in a strongly republican area. John had a rather fine, well educated south country English accent and with it he went to the bar and asked for a pint. The whole bar became totally silent, each eye moving towards this strange apparition that clearly was an Englishman. "I'll buy that man a pint!" someone cried, "He's the first Englishman ever to come into this bar!" History does not relate how many pints John actually downed that night, my guess is quite a few. Perhaps if the government had sponsored John to enter all the republican pubs in the province he might have made a real difference to the troubles.

John was at home with movers of human thought and experience, the noble and good who one day history might relate to have changed the world. But he was more at home with Richie Roche, a publican, a poacher at times, a dear friend and, in his masculine Irish red haired way, a lover of men. If ever there was a hero in John's life it was Richie. Not a great thinker in the world scene, not a person who would change the way of mankind, just a man, a friend who, as it says in the Bible, was "closer than a brother."

Richie, like his brother and their father before them, kept a pub. It was one of the smarter pubs in Duncannon, not five miles up the river from the cottage. There were some times when the place was full of youngsters and other times when they played local Irish music. Richie Roche became, and by all means would still be, a drinking partner of John's; they were the greatest of friends. Lonesome drinkers are dangerous people but those who drink together invent the world and share much more than the hours it takes to make a proper job of abusing the liver. He was taller than most, boasting a huge red beard behind which hid an infectious smile and an honest face.

One evening John and Angela's car broke down outside Dublin and it was Richie who came to the rescue. He left the pub in the hands of his children and set off to drive through the night to recover them. One of John's first encounters with Richie was when he had broken his hand. The doctors seemed not to be able to do anything for him, but Richie knew a man. Almost everyone in Ireland 'knows a man' that can do this or that. In this case it was an animal bone setter who moonlighted on humans. Richie gave John an awful lot of whiskey to cope with the pain and together they drove into the countryside. The waiting room was filled with patients similarly fortified, and more whiskey was consumed while dreadful groans and bellows came from the treatment room. John was eventually looked at. Strange and terrible screams came from behind the thin wall; then he was cured. The fact that both John and Richie had drunk more whiskey than was safe for driving highlights John's less than conventional and responsible attitude to being in charge of a motor vehicle while under the influence of alcohol. One night in Wales he drove home 'with a skinful' through the countryside to Fachongle Isaf. In the morning the car was a little knocked about.

"Do you remember hitting that bank last night?" a friend asked him later that day. "Which bank?" John looked for telltale vegetation on the car. "The Midland Bank."

Coming home from Richie's bar with a few (unpaid for) salmon on the back seat and more than a few paid for and free whiskeys surging around his veins, John was stopped by the Garda. It was sometime in the morning but not yet light.

"Good morning, Mr. Seymour."

"Good morning, officer."

"Those are fine looking salmon."
"Ah....."
"And sure you've had quite a few drinks."
"Ah...."
"And now you're driving home"
"Ah..."
"Well don't let us stop you, sure we only wanted to give you a fright!"
Smiles all round and a cheery Goodnight saw John gingerly driving off into the blackness.

John acquired a caravan which he hitched to his old Lada and he and Angela took off on a tour of Ireland. In the subsequent book *Blessed Isle, One Man's Ireland*, John explored the relationship between the ordinary people and their masters, from Norman invasion to the present day. John himself was an interloper, an Englishman living in Ireland, but like many an Irishman before him, John did not have anything good to say about Oliver Cromwell. The Lord High Protector of England gave Catholic landowners a choice either to flee over the Shannon to the boggy land of Connaught or die. They did both and the new landowners, the Protestant English, replaced them. The Churches, the Cathedrals, the whole infrastructure of the country was stolen by puritan Protestants and thousands upon thousands of families lost their lives.

John quotes letters sent back to England from observers at the time where they thank God for his hand mightily killing two thousand men, women and children here and the drowning of a similar number there. Every settlement it seemed had its own story to tell about Cromwellian harshness. But it was the decades that followed this conflict that were far worse for them. The rights of the people to their own land had been taken away. They had to rent their farms from people who thought it an almost religious right to keep Catholicism at bay by extracting the highest rents they could from the peasantry. Keeping them poor was official policy. John called it "Rack Renting". The new landowners could exact the maximum rent, almost make up a figure plucked from the air, and the people had to pay it or they would be thrown into the country lanes. This systematic oppression continued for over two hundred years and John met people even in the 1980s who still remembered being evicted for not affording the unfair rent imposed upon them.

Peasants grew crops but never ate them, kept pigs but never tasted pork, had chickens but durst not eat the eggs because everything had to be sold in order to meet the rent. The people were utterly broken. After the Battle of the Boyne the persecution of Catholics hardened. They were not allowed to own land or horses above a certain value and they were unable to leave land in their will unless the recipient was a Protestant. John found himself amazed that the population simply did not become Protestants en-masse because they had every incentive to do so and every disincentive to remain Roman Catholic. He points out that the Scots and the Welsh largely stuck to religion other than that prescribed by the English. The Scots chose Presbyterianism, the Welsh Methodism. If the English had used a more velvety glove in these lands then perhaps the United Kingdom would have remained so.

The famine years of the nineteenth century were exacerbated by the land owner system. In order to thwart the bailiff, who could easily take a stored crop such as wheat, the people took to growing potatoes. This crop could be left in the earth until it was needed and no bailiff could be bothered to dig it up. But when the potato crops were successively destroyed by a fungal infection over a period of around ten years there remained little else to eat. As a result the population of Ireland was decimated and did not recover its pre-famine numbers until nearly two hundred years later.

Will Sutherland had invited John to be a speaker at the Fourth World Conference which he organised in London in 1991. He greatly admired John's no nonsense philosophy and his zest for real living. The Rio Earth Summit of 1992 galvanised Will's desires to live in a green way and he asked permission to join John and Angela on their Killowen smallholding. He had met Angela in London a year previously. They fell in love, married and now have two children. Together, John, William and Angela started the School for Self-Sufficiency, a more organised version of the Welsh one started by John over a decade before.

John's time in Ireland was productive in terms of writing. He completed a number of re-workings of the Complete Book of Self-Sufficiency, one with Will Sutherland as co-author, as well as many others. He had, during his time of working on the Centre for Living in Wales, written furiously, mostly to earn money to furnish his debts. Here in Ireland he was secure enough to allow his writing to be less frantic, but not less productive. He started a number of pro-jects that were to make him world famous. One was a television series for the BBC, *Far from Paradise*, with a BBC book of the same title. It was pre-sented and written with Herbert Girardet, the Australian activist. Herbert remembers the time. They were not actually filmed together. Each of them presented a 'chapter' alternately and sepa-rately. John, accompanied by Angela, travelled all over the world making the film. It drew largely on John's collected knowledge of over a dozen years living with African and Indian natives and studying their husbandry. Herbert interspersed John's more practical episodes with theoretical considerations. "When we did meet, he made us all laugh. He was larger than life and at the time he was keen on haranguing the agricultural giants for poisoning the earth. He sang some great songs about them." Herbert remembers that it was quite something to make a television series and write a book together yet hardly meet.

John's health deteriorated as the century was giving way to a new millennium. His eyesight was failing him and he was finding the daily routine harder to cope with. His last book was his collected poems. As John loved to sing, many of them were written to the tunes of popular songs, such as a whole group of anti-GM, anti-nuclear, anti-planning, anti-anything not green, poems to be sung to the tune of 'My Old Man's a Dustman'. He had become famous in Ireland by giving little talks about the country and the countryside just after the news at six o'clock. His last TV appearance for RTE was to talk about writing and being a writer. He offered advice such as don't become a writer because you think it's a good job as it involved hours and hours of hard lonely work. Moreover he said that people should become writers only because they had something they desperately had to say. A helpful friend provided John with a computer which he used for writing. At length he had to print his words at the highest font size available so that it could be visible. His old typewriter, on which he had written so many books, was now no longer of use.

John's return to Wales was for some both a

wrench and a healing. A wrench because John remained loyal to Ireland and indeed to Angela and Will until the end. A healing because he was to return to the bosom of his family, to Anne and Dai and Kett. There would be Vicky Moller and the slow return of friends who could more easily get to him, and then of course, his mountain.

John returned knowing more or less it was to be his last journey. He left instructions to Will Sutherland; "If I die in Ireland bury me in the garden, if I die in Wales, bury me there." There is a memorial plaque in John's favourite piece of the garden at Killowen Cottage.

Chapter Eight
Arthurstown Seven

The multinational chemical company, Monsanto, and John Seymour had something in common although neither would admit to it. Both adhered to the truth that in order to feed the growing numbers of people on the planet the actual yield of crops per acre must increase. John would say that the Monsanto way of achieving this was by liberal use of an oil based agricultural system, the compounding of small farms into larger ones, increased mechanisation, the protection of so called intellectual copyright hidden somewhere deep in a seed and the inevitable removal of most of mankind from the agricultural process.

John's view was somewhat different. His way of increasing yield is labour intensive, low input farming that is self-sustaining, hard work and of course completely free from the attentions of chemically or genetically messed about with food. In *The Fat of the Land* he writes of a friend who farms ten thousand acres, producing just one crop - barley - and whose production is based on the use of chemicals. The land received no organic material and the output per acre was very low, but the output per man hour was very large. Taking only three men to run the farm means that *financially* it was a success. Biologically, however, it was a disaster, the soil suffering for monetary profit in a non-sustainable way. John argued that if the land was split into a thousand units of ten acres, each with a family trained to live off the land, then these ten thousand acres would become very productive indeed. Together they would produce a community of healthy people and almost as a by-product there would be a huge surplus of healthy organic food.

For the last decade of the twentieth century at least, the juxtaposing of these points of view found their focus in the GM debate.

In 1982 Monsanto scientists were the first in the world to genetically modify a plant cell and within two years the dedicated Chesterfield Life Sciences Research Centre was opened in the US to develop GM organisms. Within a dozen years, Roundup Ready Soya, Maize and Oilseed Rape were ready for commercial use. It was sold in the US and Canada, but did not have universal appeal. Anti-GM campaigners had worries about the safety of GM products to human health, to the environment and to the way we produce our food altogether. All of a sudden a seed became more than a viable germ capable of growth and of producing a crop. It had become a copyrighted library of information, possession of which was subject to contractual legality. Worries of a so called 'terminator gene' which rendered the seed infertile and incapable of being kept for sowing in the following season, were rife. What if this gene got into other crops? What if it killed bees or wildlife? Companies researching GM denied there was any such thing as 'terminator technology'.

However, the application of GM technology to other crops increased exponentially. Research was international and significant pressure was brought to bear by the American government as well as the companies involved to ensure that somehow GM organisms were introduced into as many countries as possible all over the world, even if only to test them in one way or another. Monsanto, in the fullness of time, were to ask the Environmental Protection Agency (EPA) of the Irish government to provide a licence for a field trial of GM sugar beet. The gene, spliced into sugar beet's

DNA, gave the plant increased resistance to the Monsanto Product, Roundup - a multi-purpose, systemic herbicide. The trial crop was a joint venture between Monsanto and The Irish Agriculture and Food Development Authority (TEAGASC). The site chosen was a small corner of a farm belonging to Martin Foley of Coleman, Arthurstown.

The application and subsequent granting of a licence to release the first GM genes into Ireland was widely denounced by politicians and campaigners around Ireland. The furore spilled over into the Dáil. Mr Higgings TD, representative for Dublin West, said in a debate some months later,

"It is outrageous that the Environmental Protection Agency and the previous government allowed tests by the multinational company Monsanto on sugar beet to take place in this country with no public discussion on the merits and demerits of genetic engineering."

On May 1st Justice Michael Morriarty in the High Court of Ireland granted an interim injunction to Ms. Clare Watson, a founder member of Genetic Concern, a coalition of Irish farmers, women's groups, seed savers, environmentalists and others. It prohibited the planting of GM sugar beet. According to the EPA's own report on the application, the lack of public debate was the most common complaint raised by objectors. Other complaints included fears of increased use of herbicide, gene pollution, gene transfer to weeds, as well as ethical, moral and social implications. The group, Genetic Concern, accused the Irish Government and the EPA of accepting information from companies who 'had a heavy interest in the outcome'. The injunction only lasted three weeks and as the government refused a debate in the Dáil, there was little opportunity for the public to inform themselves on the matter nor have any say about whether the trial should go ahead. It was reported in the press that Monsanto planted the crop on the same afternoon that the injunction ended.

A weekend of public trespass and direct action against the Monsanto crop was organised which coincided with a sustainable organic food fair at Duncannon Fort organised by Davie Philips. He was one of the founders of an organisation called 'Low Impact' and an organiser of the 'Sustainable Earth Fairs'. Besides John, Nuala Ahern MEP (Green Party), Joe Higgins TD (Socialist Party and member for Dublin East) and John Gormley TD (Green Party) were speaking. John Seymour was largely regarded as the godfather of self-sufficiency in Ireland and consequently was a popular speaker. He had been invited to speak at this and similar events in previous years. Davie organised a public fringe meeting to alert the locals of the dangers of genetic engineering in food and agriculture. John and the others informed the people attending of the immediate threat posed by genetically modified organisms. It was after this talk that they moved to demonstrate at the

Monsanto site. The accounts of the time lead one to believe that people simply decided to walk to the site and destroy the crop in a spontaneous manner. This is not the case at all, and it was John Seymour who was one of the main motivators towards some kind of public show of disapproval. Fifty years after the war John was a captain again.

The name Arthurstown Seven was something of a misnomer. There were many more, possibly up to seventy, who actually walked over the GM crop trial and uprooted plants. Before the day of the protest they had made sure that everyone knew where the GM crop was being grown. 'Biohazard' posters had been placed on trees, fences and road sides, so that as many people as possible knew about the site. Busses had been arranged for people to get to the Duncannon Good Food Fair and without them knowing, Monsanto had been out filming people getting on them. Perhaps naively this filming took the organisers by surprise. There had been reports that the crop had already been destroyed three days earlier.

When they arrived at the site Garda and Monsanto security guards were discretely filming and taking notes. The test crop had been destroyed as reported. Who actually did this is open to debate. It is not likely that it was John or his colleagues at the Good Food Fair, simply because they would have been spotted by security. Whether it was an attempt to wrong foot anti-GM campaigners in Ireland by Monsanto destroying their own test remains to be seen. John said it was the Fairies, but then perhaps he had better information and just wasn't letting on. All in all, John was first over the fence, followed by dozens of others. They all began to pull up what remained of the GM beet. John wrote a poem about the time:

> *The GM Fairies got it right*
> *they bashed the Beet in dead of night*
> *Monsanto's game - just one solution*
> *they had to stop this life pollution.*
> *Mutant beet we do not need*
> *Planted in Ireland just for greed.*
> *Those twisted genes for sure would spread*
> *to gardens, fields, and our daily bread.*

The whole event was good mannered. Protesters talked to Garda and explained what they were doing and why they were doing it. There were children and journalists in the open field and security guards hidden and constantly filming. It was Joe Higgins TD, Member of the Irish Parliament for the Socialist Party, later to speak against Monsanto quite openly in the House of the Oireachtas, who initially spotted the hidden cameramen. Some reports state that the Garda started to arrest John, but then decided to withdraw, and Richie Roche later said in court that he had been arrested on the site. In actual fact no one was detained by the Garda and it was many weeks before they had made their rounds and finally arrested six people and a journalist.

Of all those at the event who had pulled up plants at the test site it appears that the Garda selected who to arrest carefully. For example, it was reported that the Garda did not interview any of the politicians involved in the protest and that they simply ignored a number of people who telephoned them to admit that they were at the site and that they had pulled up sugar beet. In the end, John along with Richie Roche, Adrienne Murphy, Davie Philips, Pauric Cannon and Gavin Harte were arrested and charged with forcible entry on to Monsanto's trial site in Arthurstown on June 21st 1998, and with causing criminal damage. Freelance journalist Mr Caoimhín Woods was charged with forcible entry on to the site.

They appeared at New Ross District Court on Tuesday February 9th. Support came in from all over Ireland and Davie Phillips remembers the feeling of humility that so many people were behind them. David Bulbulia, defending solicitor and someone who did his job with great aplomb, said in his preliminary in court that the case was a complicated one and, given the fact that the state intended bringing ten witnesses and that the defence also planned to bring several expert witnesses, giving evidence would probably take two days. Judge Donnacha O'Buachalla adjourned the case until March 31 and set aside the following day so that evidence could be heard.

The seven were charged with damaging "without lawful excuse sugar beet belonging to Monsanto (Ireland) Limited, intending to damage such property or being reckless as to whether such property would be damaged" under the 1991 Criminal Damage Act. The original charge was that they had damaged "genetically modified sugar beet", but at the trial the words "genetically modified" were dropped. This was at the insistence of the Director for Public Prosecutions but why the change was necessary is not recorded. Their defence would rest in proving that they had a lawful excuse for what they did, and this was exploited to the full, not only in court but to the rest of the world.

Opposite the New Ross District Court the various organisations involved rented a hotel ballroom for the period of the trial. It was used as their base and doubled up as a venue for a two day awareness raising event about what they saw as the dangers of GM. There were idea sharing forums, informative displays, public speakers, street theatre, good healthy organic food and lots of music. They wanted to make the event as colourful and friendly as possible, putting a strong emphasis on informing people about the possible hazards of genetic engineering, and giving organic food lots of coverage as a sustainable alternative to what John described as mutant pap. In court everyone pleaded not guilty to criminal damage without lawful excuse. They all firmly believed that "GM was a serious and immediate threat to health and the environment" and therefore, according to the law, they had a lawful excuse to act as they did.

John was both eloquent and determined. He told the court,

" ...*if a government does not take action to protect its citizens from serious danger, is it not reasonable that the citizens should take action to protect themselves? If an army of Normans landed again at Baginbun and started looting and destroying I should expect the Irish army to go and try and stop them. If it did not then I should feel it my duty to go and try and stop them myself, if not with a pike then at least with a pitch fork and I should do so. And when a huge multinational corporation comes and starts planting completely untested and untried genetically mutilated plants in the country where I have made my home, and the government agencies which are supposed to be there to protect us from that sort of thing fail in their duty, then I feel it not only my right but my duty too to do something to try to stop them. And*

if I have to go to prison because of it then I will go with a
good will, and make the best of it, and when I get out I
will try to stop them again!"

His argument drew a poignant parallel with
Irish history because the Normans did indeed land
at Baginbun nine hundred years earlier. *"To mess*
around with God's creation" by fundamentally alter-
ing the makeup of plants, is a *"mortal sin, and it's a*
mortal sin, if you understand that, not to prevent it,"

Of course, Richie was deeply involved
"because John was involved" as he told me on the
telephone. It is strange that John is widely known
as the father of self-sufficiency, because in actual
fact, he was far from being self-sufficient himself.
What's more, I do not believe he ever thought of
self-sufficiency being something that left you relying on *just* yourself. For John, friendship, the kind
of friendship that led to a deep affection - even
love - was the basic currency of life. Because John
was who he was Richie simply wanted to be involved in some of John's life, because that was the
kind of man *Richie* was. When an ally was needed,
Richie was available. So it was fairly inevitable that
when Davie Philips, John and Adrienne Murphy
were looking for co-protestors, Roche's Bar was
the perfect place to start and at times Richie's pub
became unofficial HQ.

John was quite prepared to go to prison if
necessary. He was determined that he would not

pay Monsanto a penny of the sixteen thousand pounds they were demanding, quite a lot for a quarter of an acre's worth of sugar beet even if it was genetically modified. But in all the trial, its build up and all the surrounding pressures that go with it, John remained a party animal - albeit an eighty four year old party animal with increasing blindness and marked deafness. Adrienne Murphy remembers him as being the group's morale offi-cer. His easy approach to life and what was going on around him rubbed off on the others and eased their fears.

Adrienne Murphy, described by John as the glamour element of the group, was vilified by Kevin Myers in the Irish Times in a tirade against what he saw as colonial ideas trying to stop Ireland making progress in an important area of science. Adrienne is an environmentalist, writer and jour-nalist based in Dublin. She described John as a hero and one of the highlights of her life was to receive from him a signed copy of his book *Playing it for laughs, a Book of Doggerel.* They met to discuss strat-egy either at John's home or in a pub - frequently Roche's Bar. On one occasion, Adrienne remem-bers, "Despite the seriousness of the occasion spir-its in the pub were extremely high as they always were when John - one of the most vivacious, hi-larious and extroverted people that I've ever met - decided to party." Perhaps one of the most accu-rate descriptions of the time were recorded in

Adrienne's obituary for John in the Irish Times.

"*During our trial preparation, while the rest of us frantically researched the scientific hazards associated with GM - trying to prove that we were compelled to break the law in order to prevent GM contamination - John just laughed, utterly confident in his simple defence that he had acted to protect God's creation. John was very much the ringleader of the GM damage, and it was incredibly reassuring during the stress of the trial to have someone so wise and funny and calm around. Even Monsanto, with all their cash and political clout and big bully tactics of spying, hadn't a hope in hell of intimidating this brave and noble man. John would gladly have gone to prison for a year over the GM issue. No doubt he would've made a lot of new friends, because people loved him wherever he went.*"

A number of witnesses were brought before the judge by the prosecution. Among them an Environmental Protection Agency scientific officer. Dr Tom McLoughlin, spoke about the issuing of the original licence to grow the crop. Among more than 3,500 representations from the public about five GM crop trials licensed by the EPA were concerns about "unpredictable technology" and risk of "superweeds"; and the belief that GM genes would spread to wild species or cross-

pollinate with other plants. Monsanto's belief was
that the chance of cross-pollination or genetic contamination from GM sugar beet was very low.
When he was asked to comment on the fact that
they only had Monsanto's data to prove this he said
that this was how it was done in the EU and in
other countries. It is not recorded if he was asked
if he thought this was a proper way of going about
things in Ireland.

In a magical piece of compromise, the
judge applied the Probation Act to six of the seven
the defendants. This was a face saving and somewhat non-committal way out for all. Found guilty
but basically let off. Monsanto didn't get their sixteen thousand pounds but were able to say that
they had the right of legality on their side. However, what the judge actually said was important.
Firstly he recognised that the whole protest had
taken place in a good-natured way, with no chal-
lenge to the authority of the Gardai.

It was also recognised that these people did
what they did in the full view of everyone. The
fact that they had been secretly filmed went in
their favour. An organisation called Gaelic Earth
Liberation Front (GELF) had been going around
the countryside destroying crops in secret, but this
has never been John Seymour's way of doing
things. The judgement noted the honest intentions
of the protesters. What they did, they did upfront,
and their actions can be judged according to

their merits.

The defendants had the opportunity to tell Ireland about GM - which they did with a great deal of verve. Morally they maintained that they were right, and although the judge could not agree that it was right to go around destroying other people's property, he was certainly not inclined to throw the book at them. Of course the majority of the public agreed with them.

The whole process ended in warm humour in a way only possible in Ireland. Before sentencing it is customary for any previous convictions to be read out. This took only a few minutes for everyone, except Richie Roche. Richie, described as the 'town heretic' by Davie Philips, had a number of previous convictions. For one thing this meant that the Probation Act did not apply in his case. He was bound over to keep the peace. Among his convictions he had been 'caught in possession of a salmon', had been arrested for having a small amount of ammunition on his person and had a number of licensing convictions. A loveable rogue, right in John's good books!

Chapter Nine

A Party and a Planting

John entered the digital revolution kicking and screaming when a friend bought him a computer. He really needed it because, without the ability to choose the largest point size on his word processor, he couldn't actually see the words. By 2002 his health was not good despite the odd statement found in the press or on self-sufficiency bulletins that extolled him to be nearly ninety and doing just as much as he was when he was younger.

The truth was somehow different. He was almost blind and worsening deafness was becoming a problem. More ominously, he had prostrate cancer, his diet was deteriorating and he was beginning to get himself into a state. He had a number of hospital appointments that, for one reason or another, he found himself unable to keep and if this continued he was in danger of ending up being beyond help.

Intestinal adhesions are caused by areas of scar tissue which can cause the gut and other internal organs to stick together. Most people would not even know they had abdominal scar tissue. In a small number of people who have adhesions, John included, the fibrous bands of scar tissue block the flow of material through the intestines either completely or partially. This blockage is called an intestinal obstruction and it can lead to death. He suffered repeatedly from this and always in the back of the mind was the worry that it might lead to something more serious. In these cases it is not uncommon for the bowel to block and then re-open, leading to repeated bouts of obstruction and consequent agonising pain.

It was decided that John should go home to Wales to live with Anne and David and so he crossed the Irish Sea, this time without the almost compulsory singing and drinking that marked so many of his trips to the 'Blessed Isle.' His arrival was preceded by a great deal of activity. There were many alterations needed to make the place ready for John. Vicky Moller helped Anne and David with a loan to cover the cost of the work. They made a single room into a home for John

with a double windowed door to see his favourite
sight, the Mountain of Angels. It had a wood burning fire and John's books were spread all around.
On a second wall another door led to a pantry and
the room housed the best shower I've ever seen in
a private house.

The elaborately tiled shower room has two
windows, one to the garden where you can sit on
the toilet and gaze at people toiling away, and the
other to the mountain. John could walk, so he had
no trouble making his way around the house, although he found it difficult to actually see. Anne
made his room beautiful with art, hangings, car-
pets and curtains. It became a refuge for many
more people than John. On the wall opposite the
bed were two paintings by William Seymour of the
Broom, with the children playing contentedly on
the lawn outside the part of the house where Anne
and Kate were born and which later became Sally's
pottery.

John arrived, along with his books and not
much else. Hillaire Beloc, Tony Benn, Karl Marx,
dozens of farming books, Bibles, encyclopaedias,
books on the environment, books on peace, books
on Africa and India, repair manuals, guide books,
poetry books, books, books. And there was John.
Largely the same John, only tired. One gets the
feeling that his time here was among his happiest
days. In many ways they were idyllic. Old friends
trickled back to see him and, as far as possible with

someone who was ill, Anne and David introduced a great sense of peace into their surroundings.

John took to sleeping in the afternoon except for his trips to hospital. His cancer did not bother him that much except he had some pain in his legs. The only place that could offer him radiotherapy was a hospital in Swansea. Daily visits made a round trip of four hours, which was tiresome but completed just the same. It is ironic that the science that created nuclear weapons, 'Megadeaths' as he described them, was the same science that was now fighting to keep him alive. The 'men in white coats' now had friendly faces. His age and his cancer as well as the treatment would take their toll, but generally he was a model patient. David remembers those long drives with John, hardly able to see, mistaking every large building for a catholic Church.

John tried, whenever he could, to be active and actually do something for a part of each day. He would take a stroll around the few acres of David and Anne's home, the garden or the poly-tunnels. He picked the odd bucket of fruit or flowers for wine making, although this was not all that successful. Gorse flower wine was difficult. Whenever the gorse flower is blooming, it is then designated as kissing season. The fact that the gorse flowers in every month of the year makes kissing a very popular pastime. John's eyesight had deteriorated so much that picking gorse just made his fingers bloody - so he turned to oak leaf wine instead.

Sally turned up on April 12th 2004 and Vicky Moller lived just down the road. All of a sudden John was surrounded by wives and doting women. It is true that every one of the women in his life continued to love him, despite periods of anger or jealousy. Sally would read to him - mostly his own books and they would relive the times together, laughing, crying a little but mostly falling asleep. Of course, John's illness did not remove from him the enjoyment of his 'reasonable refreshment'. He was frequently in high spirits, was always looking out for a glass of something and always ready to continue living in his usual way - being great fun. His favourite drink was a 'sundowner' which I suppose was a glass of whiskey drunk at sundown. But then, when you were nearly blind, the sun could be going down at any time!

Preparations for the big party day, John's 90th birthday, were long in the making. Sally helped with encouragement, energy and knowledge - there were more than a hundred guests to be remembered and contacted, and pure physical hard work. All the grass was cut, the open shed emptied and cleaned out for the food area, a marquee erected for musicians and drinks and people should it rain. Fortunately the weather was kind on the 12th June. People arrived early to help out, and many of them just started to party instead of helping. However, due to the good weather most of the jobs were done on time.

To avoid a tedious list of booze, suffice it to say there was a considerable volume and variety of liquid. The quantities of intoxicating beverages consumed brought major problems for the plumbing at the little house. Their system would simply not cope with the expected tsunami of human waste so a stand alone portaloo was erected with a sign on the door instructing gentlemen to make full use of the surrounding countryside. Richie Roche and his wife Eileen brought a friend from Ireland on a 'raiding party'. Richie sparked off a great deal of merriment with John as always; they remembered their times together in Ireland and drank freely for a while. Richie brought whiskey and straight away attacked the whole lamb that Sally was spit roasting. A pit had been dug and filled with wood and an improvised spit was lain over the hole to cook the animal on. She was not amused, the meat was not fully cooked, but this did not deter Richie's frequent raiding.

John loved the party but it was tiring and he couldn't get round everyone. Normally used to a good afternoon nap, he had so many people to talk to that he simply did not have the chance to sleep. People who could not manage to get there on the day came on the next, and the next and so it was reported that they were partying for a whole week, which they probably were on and off. He had consumed his family birthday present quite early, two dozen oysters and a lobster. John's favourite food was not to the taste of the rest of his family, indeed they remained ever bemused by his penchant for them. The oyster shells now adorn the edges of his grave.

John was overjoyed by his cake, with some fireworks snorting away out of it, and following kisses and speeches and hundreds of hands shaken came the long and generous task of talking again to many friends, each of them important not because they were a part of the 'great man's' past but because they lived and breathed and were a part of John's or his family's lives. That is how they made people welcome, you just became one of them, not sucked into a character greater than yourself, simply accepted. In a way this was John's greatest success and possibly his greatest gift to the world. He simply accepted people, well those who were not trying to blow the place up or poison it or change the genetics of living things. John Papworth described this ability to make people feel important, even loved, as "a great generosity of spirit" and it seems to be a trait passed on to his children.

Evening came and a great log fire was started around which people sat and sang in an easy group. The evening gave way to night and guests simply slept everywhere and anywhere, a sleep lubricated by a considerable volume of alcohol, food and merriment. Sleep would have come easily. The morning scene was one of sleeping bags filled with bodies in the house, on all the floors, the kitchen, the lawn, the shed and the beer tent. For a few days the place resembled the Centre for Living - a chaotic mass of humanity, slightly dazed, dishevelled and hungry. But there were no fields to plough, no pigs to feed, just a few eggs to collect and to wait in turn for a much needed cup of tea. Others arrived and the process began again, repeating itself with minor changes for a few days. No new cake, fewer friends, longer conversations, more family.

Eventually everything was over and life returned to normal - hospital visits resumed, as did afternoon naps. This was a special time for John and Sally and she stayed until late August before leaving for Ireland to spend a fortnight with their daughter Jane. During this time John sang a lot. He played the melodeon - badly according to Alan Waller- otherwise his love for folk music might have seen him travelling the country playing folk tunes in Pubs. He taught Owen, Anne and David's son, his favourite song, The Oyster Girl - the twinkle in John's eye becoming more culinary than anything else.

As I was a walking down a London Street,
A pretty little Oyster Girl I chanc-ed for to meet,
She was neat and she was pretty from her top-knot to her
feet,
And she bargained for a basket of oysters.
Oh Oysters, oh oysters, oh oysters she cried,
I have the finest oysters that ever you espied,
I'll sell them ten a penny but twelve I'll sell to thee,
If you'll bargain for a basket of oysters.

Oh landlord, oh landlord, oh landlord I cried,
Have you got a little room for the Oyster Girl and me,
Where we can sit together and merry, merry be,
While I bargain for a basket of oysters.

We weren't in the room for half and hour or more,
That pretty little oyster girl she opened up the door,
She picked all my pockets and down the stairs she fled,
And she left me with a basket of oysters.

Oh landlord, oh landlord, oh landlord I cried,
Did you see that little Oyster Girl a sitting by my side,
She picked all my pockets and the landlord he replied,
Well you shouldn't have been so fond of your oysters.

> *Now all you brisk young men be advised by me,*
> *If you happen to have an Oyster Girl a sitting on your*
> *knee,*
> *First lock the door - then take away the key,*
> *Or she'll leave you with a basket of oysters.*

It was clear from this time onward that John's health was deteriorating and that he was becoming more frail. He was catheterised, sometimes with the bag attached to a frame which he carried around. "Meet the wife!" he would frequently joke. But then the jokes faded away. He found it more difficult to get around. He wrote to Sally, his first real love, asking her to be happy, and perhaps to come back to live in Wales. John always regretted the break up of their marriage. He had told John Papworth some time previously that if he had stayed with Sally, everything would have been fine.

After the birthday celebrations Sally prepared to return to Australia. She planned to break her journey by visiting a friend in Canada. When in Toronto Sally had a massive stroke and was not expected to live. The rest of the family, apart from Anne and David, dashed out to be with her: Jane and Kate from Australia and Dai from Wales - and Rhiannon, Jane's daughter, the oldest grandchild. They had to make decisions - should Sally be resuscitated if she had another stroke? One decision they made easily was not to tell John.

Anne, David and John talked about the details of what was to happen following his passing. He wanted to be buried, and everyone knew where, but his major concern was that he had a green burial. *"I want the worms to get to me quick!"* He gave instructions for his cardboard coffin to be drilled with holes so that he could become a part of the ecosystem as quickly as possible. David prevaricated a little about ordering the coffin. Eventually John's final decision to simply let nature take its course was a spiritual one. He was adamant about his passing - *"I've travelled three continents, I've written forty books, I've done enough on this planet, I want to die"*.

Friends were contacted once it became clear that John was close to death. Most of the family were in Canada and couldn't really get back and abandon Sally, consequently they missed John's passing. Richie Roche and Eileen came over. "Jesus!" he said, "I have never seen a man so close to death!" When they had to return, Richie reassured John with "I'll see you on the other side!" Maybe to many this simple statement might sound a little clichéd, but between these two great friends it had a special meaning. It helped John a lot; strangely even in John's final days, Richie was helping him on a journey like so many times before.

The room where John stayed was still and quiet except for the low conversations around him

and with him. People would come in and read to
him, sometimes with response, other times without. Early one morning David caught John's eye as
it opened, "How long does it take to die?" They
both smiled. The cardboard coffin was ordered and
the district nurse was frequently in attendance.
John had twice been given the last rights of the
Catholic Church, an event appreciated not only by
himself but some days later by Angela.

John's death was one of those spiritual mo-
ments that can only be shared by people who have
watched someone die. Impossible to describe,
death can be a release, a final statement of humanity, a sort of communication between everyone
involved that promoted a feeling of well being,
that all is well and right. It isn't closure because the
dead are always with us, perhaps even more so
than the living in our memories and our fondest
places. Anne noted that John's wrinkles disappeared and he looked at peace. Coincidentally, the
doctor was present at his time of passing, and it
was her first encounter with actual death. Mostly
she had been called after the event, and she was
clearly moved. Death does not always have to be a
bad experience.

Others had to be told. The family still bat-
tling it out in Canada, the Ashe family, many
friends. The first friend to be contacted was John
Papworth, who was heartbroken. Then there was
Richie. His wife answered the telephone. Richie

was out playing golf. She was able to contact him and ring Anne with their immediate response. "He's sober with grief!"

The doctor was not moved enough, however, to issue a Death Certificate. Regulations and general medical nervousness following the Harold Shipman affair compelled her to decline issue once she realised that John was to be buried at home. Both she and the nurse were surprised to hear that there were to be no undertakers involved and no chapel of rest. John had moved away from home enough; he was now staying put. It was David's job to run around officialdom to obtain the proper documentation to get John's final event underway. With what he thought were the correct papers assembled, David tried to register the death. He appeared at the registry office with John's Birth Certificate and the newly appropriated Death Certificate. After the official condolences were over the Registrar asked David if he had John's Birth Certificate, "It makes it all so much easier." But she was not too happy when she inspected both documents. The Death Certificate bore the name John Seymour, whereas the Birth Certificate named him John Turbayne; It took several minutes of head scratching to work out what to do next. "I know," she said. "When I ask you if you have got the Birth Certificate, you say 'No!'" So she did ask David for the said document, and he said he didn't have it, and that was that.

People began to arrive for the funeral. John Papworth was to lead the affair, and since John was at home and not in a refrigerated Chapel of Rest, everyone knew they only had a few days at most to bury him. The room where he lay was opened, windows and doors, anything to cool it down. The District Nurse knew little of rigor mortis. Most people went to the undertaker straight away and David had to explain what was happening to John's body as well as forcibly dress him, helped by his closest family. David also had to explain the processes to various officials by which a person comes to be interred on his own land. When we slept in the room in which John died, the 'Home Funeral' book was on the shelves, nestled between John's books.

A steady stream of friends came and went to pay their respects to John. He was buried in his suit, a silk handkerchief in his breast pocket. He was known for his red or blue spotted handkerchief. He had some personal items in his pockets, a bottle of Holy Water with the liquid replaced with poteen, a pocket knife, a silver shilling, some string, his 'Wexfork Pike' badge, some soil from his garden, a poem from Angela, an acorn and he was ready. Except he wasn't ready because the cardboard coffin had not arrived. Someone at the factory was sick or on holiday, but the family could not delay matters further.

The place where they buried him was described by John a dozen years earlier in *The Blessed Isle*. It looks up from the highest point of his old farm towards the mountain that he would climb, sometimes drunk and sometimes sober. They dug the hole, and where his head would rest they found a large piece of bluestone, the same material he had spent digging out of the ground or blowing up during his time at Fachongle Isaf. This became his headstone, at present unmarked and unnamed, natural and fitting the landscape like so many thousand Pembrokeshire burials in ancient times.

John's burial, or his planting as he would have put it, was even more natural than planned. Everything had to be made up as they went along and decisions were taken about what to do by most of the family, including Sally. Without a coffin it was decided to take John to his resting place on a bier made by David. He was wrapped simply in woollen blankets made from sheep he had on the Pembrokeshire farm before he left for Ireland. On top of this a hand sewn quilt was laid, bought for him as a present by Helen for his ninetieth birthday. It was bought in Goa and was beautifully embroidered with tiny mirrors covering it. They had some fun wondering how the scene would look when future generations of archaeologists dug John up in the name of science, covered with dozens of tiny mirrors, the cloth having rotted away over the years. His head was lain on a cushion from Kate. The photographs of the burial clearly showed gaps

where John's body could be seen. Hs head was un-
covered at the top, just his face was hidden. John
certainly didn't have to worry about the worms,
they were to have quick and easy access.

With John Papworth officiating, many people spoke at the graveside. John compared the
great man to characters from Shakespeare. There
was something of Hamlet in him; he knew the
deep tragedy hidden in people's lives. There was
something of the Romeo in him, ever looking for
his Juliet. There was something of the Falstaff in
him, with his love of merriment and a good rowdy
drink with friends. Above all John Seymour was
his own man bent on love. He expressed love in
many ways, and was surrounded by love at the
end. John personalised an adaptation of the prayer
of St Frances of Assisi.

Lord make me an instrument of the war against evil,
Where there is vandalism against Thy creation
Let me campaign to stop it,
Where there is sabotage of Thy genetic ordainings,
Let me fight like hell to prevent it.

Where there is conspiracy to dominate Thy world with
boardroom greed,
Let me join with others to wage an unremitting struggle
to oppose it.

*Where giant political forces combine with money makers
and pocket liners to assume control of community concerns such as education, health, commerce, banks, law
and order and work,*
*Let me be quick to affirm the overriding need for such
matters to be restored to local community life so that Thy
moral laws may prevail.*
*Where there is passivity, deference and conformism to the
powers of darkness which are degrading society and its
individual members, let me be a powerful witness to oppose them.*

*Divine master, grant that I may not so much seek to live
a quiet life as to be in the vanguard of those who would
enhance life, not so much to grab as to give, not to evade
my social obligations as to shoulder them, not to be
afraid of power as to be imbued with courage with others
to control it for worthy ends.*

*For it is in striving to act with love that we affirm love,
and in devoting ourselves to noble causes we are re-
deemed, and in giving ourselves utterly to the service of
truth, love and beauty in shared, fully democratic communities we rise to the life immortal.*

Helen, John and Frances Hurdle's daughter,
said that her time with him was short but precious.
She chose not to dwell on anything other than the
fate that matched her with this brief union of love

that was their time together. She was proud to possess half of John's genes and that if she was half as spirited, brave, forward thinking and clever as her father, she would be truly blessed.

Anne spoke on behalf of the whole family, most of whom could not be there. Sally and his daughter Kate, Dai who would have played the whistle, Rhiannon who would have sung 'The Last Rose of Summer', and Jane, who would have been beautiful and bossy, would have organised everyone and everything, and who would have spoken as well. Anne went on:

John had a lot of wives, and children. He treated them all badly and loved them. They were all devoted to him — and still are.

He inspired millions without really knowing why. But cared passionately about the important things in life, like looking after our planet — and having a good time doing it.

He was a raconteur, friend, enemy, lover, drunkard, philosopher, poet and adventurer. He was hopelessly romantic but a master of common sense and wisdom. He roared through life with the heart of an elephant, and the courage of a lion. He lived enormously — and had a beautiful death.

It has been a hell of an experience being his daughter, and an honour. And John — I thank you.

Suleman, John's neighbour and friend who owns a tree nursery just a walk away from Fachongle Isaf, wrote and read a poem for John and Will Sutherland read one of his own poems, a doggerel similar to the style of John's *Playing it for Laughs*. Vicky Moller spoke of the 'green giants' of whom John was foremost. She spoke of politics and the environmental movement that John had spearheaded or to which he had added his weight. But then she also spoke of gratitude. One of the highlights in her life was to experience the love that made John's last room such a comfortable place. She was grateful for having been a part of John's life and to David and Anne too for this final blessing they had given him. Vicky, having said her piece, slipped away to make tea and food for everyone and people returned when they felt ready to the house, leaving John alone with his mountain.

It wasn't long before the obituary machine got into full gear. They appeared in all the broadsheets and a number of magazines. They appeared in a number of Irish newspapers, and the Irish TV ran a feature on him. Most of them talked about his smallholding life, his work for the BBC and the books. The more enlightened of them talked tentatively of his family but no one with any accuracy.

167

Possibly because his personal life was so complex and so easily misunderstood, many of them got it wrong, either out of respect for John or just because they simply didn't know the truth.

Sally was holding her own in hospital but couldn't move, being paralysed on one side, and she did not have any speech. She spent a month in Toronto and was then flown back to the UK. She spent some time in hospital in Wales, where she broke her leg in a fall. This was not diagnosed for ten weeks. Unable to communicate properly, she did not make it known that she was in terrible pain. This ordeal took some considerable time to sort out. Eventually she needed further hospitalisation and now lives with Anne and David, just as John had hoped in his last letter to her. She receives constant care from her family, augmented by daily visits from nurses and carers. It is painful to compare the Sally before her problems to the Sally of today, stroke is such a dreadful illness. At the time of writing she makes steady, peaceful progress.

Chapter Ten
A World premier

The news filtered through, mostly via the internet, that John had died. There were a number of newspaper articles and the small farming press ran obituaries. It is intriguing that a low tech occupation such as digging the soil should have a high tech support system underpinning it. Smallholders who farm their land organically, who wouldn't hurt a square inch of God's earth, find themselves using a huge international computer network, employing hundreds of thousands of people, to find out how to skin a rabbit or how to treat a hen or gather a thousand other gems of information. Smallholders buy supplies on the internet, they buy *farms* on the internet, they look at smallholdings in other countries and sell their excess produce all over the world.

The Seymours were the main topic of interest on the smallholding internet sites. A number of people were remembering times when they met John, and of course there was a lot of talk about his books.

On the whole you will read about John's Dorling Kindersley books, the world famous self-sufficiency guides, and how these have been very useful. Nearly everyone confessed to having *The Complete Book of Self-Sufficiency*. They told stories of how the meat pages had blood on them and the brewing pages had wine stains on them. John was being remembered, being used as an example of noblesse in the smallholding world, and generally venerated in some way or another. From time to time some people mentioned the other books. *The Fat of the Land* and *The Hard Way to India* were favourites. A lot of people wondered what happened to Sally: Was she still alive? Were she and John still together? Since the later versions of the Dorling Kindersley books had details of the School of Self-Sufficiency in Ireland, a number of people had been there and shared their experiences online. Without exception, behind the formality of the written word appeared a warm glow of compliments. You imagine people smiling about John, even if they didn't know him.

The news of John's death had filtered through to the members of a web site called www.acountrylife.com, or ACLers as they like to be known. It is one of the more popular visiting places for smallholders who use the internet. They have little badges with ACL printed on them so that they can recognise each other and sometimes they arrange member 'get togethers' at agricultural shows or in their homes. The membership of this site is international; there are a large number from France, a currently popular destination for those wishing their own share of the country idyll. There are a large number of people who live in urban settings. Indeed, there are over five million, according to a recent survey for the *Independent* newspaper who are seriously thinking of selling up and moving to a house in the country with a few acres. The fact that '*The Complete Book of Self-Sufficiency*' was sold to non smallholders by the thousands bears this out, and the book even has the subtitle "*A practical guide for realists and dreamers*". There are many dreamers, perhaps fewer realists.

Various notices of condolence were posted on the ACL notice board, and then someone sent in John's poem Envoi which ends with the lines,

So now my friends and hearties
'Tis time to say "Farewell"
And I'll either see ye's up above
Or possibly down in Hell.

And when I finally topple over
I don't want ye's to cry
If ye's don't have a jolly good ****-up
I'll haunt ye's 'til ye die!

It was decided among the members of ACL that they had better do as John requested. After all, who wants to be haunted, even if it was someone as merry as John? The world's first international online wake was held for John Seymour on Saturday 2nd October 2004. For the whole week before there was a lot of activity. People posted messages to say they would be there, shared a few reminiscences and set up some ground rules to make it the kind of thing John would have gone to himself. It had to be alcoholic, and you had to sing a song, send in a poem or give some anecdote. Members would have their typing proficiency challenged to the maximum as the alcohol took its toll. News of the event somehow found its way into the newspapers - the Daily Mail and the Western Mail did features on what was happening, and it was even mentioned on the BBC.

Someone contacted John's family about the event, and news of Sally's condition was made public. It seems that everyone who has read *The Fat of the Land* has a soft spot for Sally and there were many who were hungry for news of how she was doing . Most of the updates that were given about Sally came from Anne Seymour.

The night of the wake appeared. In actual fact the wake lasted for nearly 24 hours because there were people signing in and raising a glass from different time zones, Australia, Canada and around Europe. Anne and Jane Seymour both managed to get online for most of the night. They were great fun, and we are led to believe they were both drinking elderflower wine. Jane was at home in Ireland and Anne in Pembrokeshire, and there broke out between them an argument about who was the more bossy. It took David, Anne's husband, to clear the matter up, saying that John would agree that Jane was by far the bossiest of the Seymour clan.

Typical of drunks wherever you meet them, in a pub on the street or even on the internet, you meet people who want to put the world to rights. Our wake started early by debating the true nature of self-sufficiency. Some said that John was not self-sufficient because he was really a professional author. But then another quoted John, saying he once described self-sufficiency as "the acceptance of complete responsibility for what you do or what you do not do." But then others, myself included, argued that self-sufficiency was not the same as self-reliance. Being apart from other humans, not relying on others for your own survival was counter to human evolution so far, which had rather become dependent on our working together for survival. This is the crux of all green thinking, that humans are a social animal and this has to be our main, some would say only, asset in dealing with the mammoth problems confronting us. John's manifesto ended with a plea to just two people, himself and his reader, to start to change the world. But even two make a partnership, a social contract, and of course there are actually more than two of us.

The deep tautologies that make such alcohol fuelled conversations barely understandable were broken by someone sending a message about their favourite passages in John's books. These included:

"Barley has two principle purposes......one is feeding animals, the other is making BEER."

"The true herdsman will find that every enterprise on his holding, if it is correctly planned, will interact beneficially with every other."

"If you had 5 acres of good well-drained land, you could support a family of 6 people and have occasional surpluses to sell."

"If you leave a hen alone, and the fox doesn't get her, she will wander off into the hedgerows and wander back again in a few weeks with a dozen little chicks clucking at her heels. These chicks being utterly naturally reared, will be the healthiest little chicks you ever will see."

Rome was not built in a day, and Rome was probably not worth building. A sound self-sufficient smallholding certainly is."

"I have found that there is only one teacher for difficult things: necessity. I milked Brownie because I had to milk her. I believe there is no other way to learn to milk a cow.....It is no use calling on the Lord God. He won't come down and help you. You are alone - with a cow.' That's true of so many things - you can go on courses and read books but in the end you just have to get on with it!"

"We never sell anything that we produce here, except Sally's pots, my writing and the occasional calf. For this we discovered early....once you start selling the produce of the land you enter the world of thieves and rogues and bounders in which you just cannot breathe. I know people who sell lettuces at a farthing when lettuces are selling in the shops- days old and stale and weary- at

ten-pence. We wish to be included out of that world,
please....."

Anne posted some of the words she spoke at
the funeral, which were touching, and it seemed,
for a moment at least, everyone was quiet. Of
course, for Jane Seymour, this small formality was
the first wake she had attended for her father because she had been in Canada looking after Sally,
and she did not have first hand knowledge of what
had happened when John was buried. People
around the world were privileged to read on their
computer screens intimate details of something
innately private, something between sisters.

People continued with messages of good will
and after a time, those who had stuck it out started
to get a bit raucous, if you can call it that. It was a
bit like those films showing children in the Australian outback who were able to join in with lessons
with classmates hundreds of miles apart thanks to
wireless radio, only this version was an internet
pub crawl. People were virtually stoned in a vir-
tual environment, probably a first that John would
have been proud of. People started to boast about
their prowess with home brew, and how it was
affecting them and then one of the Seymours set
off a sky rocket. Someone, many hundreds of miles
away, swore that at that moment they could see
the rocket through their own window and from
then on it just got silly. As bottles emptied and

eyes began to close around the world, one by one people began to shut down their computers. Oblivious to all of it was John, in his bed at the foot of his mountain, or was he? I don't know, I'm a stranger there myself.

Chapter Eleven
The Smell of New Grasses

I make no apology for including a chapter about Sally in a book that is almost exclusively about John. The reason for this is that it could be argued that, without Sally, John would not have been able to develop into the writer he was. Secondly, John managed to hoodwink so many of his readers into thinking that they were together when in actual fact they were not. It was not until 1992 and the publication of the book *Blessed Isle, One Man's Ireland,* that John let it be known that his marriage had split up, and that he had gone to live in Ireland. Until then he infers that he was still with Sally. Writing in 1978 for the second edition of the book *On My Own Terms* John writes:

"Then I lived on five acres of Suffolk ground, with Sally and our daughters Jane and Anne and Kate... Then we moved to Wales, and I have told that story in I'm a Stranger Here Myself. In our different ways we are both happy. Only sometimes I remember. I remember the smell of the new grasses..".

He is, in December 1978, inferring that he and Sally are still together. But already he had had two other partners, Frances Hurdle and Vicky Moller, with whom he had been blessed with two children, Helen and Kett, respectively. John still centred his life, in print at least, around Sally. Perhaps this was because he thought it was the right thing to do publicly, as though he thought his readers would have been put off by his lifestyle choices? Perhaps, in reality, she was still the real driving force in his life? When he wrote these words he was living in Ireland with Angela Ashe, with whom he enjoyed a special relationship. Some of John's friends, such as John Papworth, whom John confided in at the time, give us a glimpse of the mind of the man living in Ireland. He deeply loved Angela in a unique way, and was to spend the remainder of his active life there in Ireland.

Later, whenever John wrote of Sally, it was always with affection. Some of the details of Sally's life can be found in the relevant chapters of this book and, of course in John's writings, and are not repeated in this chapter.

John was not the first influence in her life with regard to self-sufficiency. Her parents had a friendship with Eric Gill, the enormously famous English sculptor and font designer. Gill Sans and Perpetua are two fonts that everyone with a computer will recognise; they were both cut in the early years of the last century and this book, by way of homage, has been typed in Perpetua. Gill Sans became famous as the typeface used by British Railways on their public signs and notices.

Gill led a colourful life and certainly the less savoury aspects of his existence as detailed in a very frank biography by Fiona MacCarthy, had nothing to do with Sally's family. But Gill also had ideals about frugal living and self-sufficiency. He rented an almost derelict convent in Wales where he and a number of families lived off the land as a community. Eric himself concentrated on his work, and was hugely influential in British art circles, but others grew the food they all ate and this way of life must have had an impact on Sally's parents. How much he influenced Sally herself is unknown.

Frank Medworth, Sally's father, was a painter, engraver, teacher of drawing, painting and wood engraving. He taught at Westminster Art School and Hull College of Art and in 1939 became head (lecturer-in-charge) of the National Art School in Sydney, Australia. His work is widely acclaimed in Australian art circles, and wider afield. Muriel Medworth, Sally's mother, was one of thirty-three artists invited to contribute a textile design to the Modern Age Fabrics exhibition in 1947, organised by Claudio Alcorso. She was a fashion and textile designer. Sally had had some success with book illustration in Australia before she came to work in the UK. She illustrated the book *Churinga Tales: Stories of Alchuringa - The Dreamtime of the Australian Aborigines* which was highly commended in the 1951 Australian Children's Book of the Year Awards. She had also illustrated a cook book before moving back to her young childhood home, England. She started working with some Australian potters, decorating pots for the Festival of Britain, after which she started throwing and decorating her own.

John described her as being one of the best pottery decorators in London. She always had a kiln nearby and her handy work provided a very steady source of income all her life. It certainly got them through a bad time on the farm, or helped pay for domestic assistance when it was needed. Art courses in the UK still refer to Sally and her work, particularly illustrative art. The largest thrust of her illustration efforts was when working with John. She was the illustrator of many of his books, the earliest being *The Fat of the Land* and continuing long after their marriage break up; the jacket design etching for *On My Own Terms* was completed in 1980, and her largest work was for the Dorling Kindersley *The Complete Book of Self-Sufficiency*. John wrote that without her the book would not have been written.

The Bohemian world of London included artists, musicians and writers as well as the general popular culture. John was not particularly inter-ested in so called popular culture and was already 40 years old. He did not describe himself as good looking, describing himself as "being no Tarzan". It is said that you can woo a woman in three ways, by being stunningly good looking, by being good at talking or by being good at listening. John pos-sessed two of these three attributes, and was not uninteresting in his own right, being a published writer, making regular contributions to the BBC, and to cap it all his publishers met in the rather select gentlemen's clubs in London, and though this cut no ice with John, in a world of would be artists that was no mean thing.

He met Sally who was living in a basement of her mother's home in Hammersmith in 1954. He fell instantly in love. He had been living on his 'double decker' which he mistakenly called, in one of his books, a 'trolley bus'. He was in the middle of a busy life, writing and researching, recording and travelling. Sally was already in a relationship when they met, and John asked her to finish it and marry him. This must have been quite something for John, who had moved around the world quite independently and seemed to show no interests in marriage, although he did show a healthy interest in women. She managed to resist his attentions for some time, but when her boyfriend went away on a trip John became particularly persistent. Sally eventually gave in.

Their initial lives together were passed in Hammersmith, but soon they bought a boat, *Jenny the Third*, in which they were to explore the inland and coastal waterways of much of England. *Jenny the Third* was a metal hulled Dutch smack, a fishing or cargo boat that had all but disappeared from their east coast home of a hundred years ago. They managed their trip with their first child Jane quite well save for a few rough times in storms. In the fullness of time they unfortunately sank *Jenny the Third*, sold her and moved on to the Broom. A subsequent move to Wales was not happy, ending in tears and separation. John and Sally had split up and John entered a difficult period. He was to set up the Centre for Life, a haphazard organisation which nearly broke him financially if not emotionally. A visitor to the farm at that time described Sally to be in a bad mood, not welcoming and difficult. She was, unknown by the visitor, going through a hard time herself.

Whether she agreed with the Centre for Life or not is not recorded, but it became necessary for John to remove her from her farm. She had to be bought out. This must have been terribly depressing for her and would explain her reaction to newcomers. She was certainly well known for her hospitality.

With the funds that came from the sale of her part of the farm, Sally moved to another a few miles away, taking Dai and Kate with her. Everything that John had written down in books, Sally had been putting into practise from day to day. She kept a house cow, pigs, chickens, grew potatoes and plenty of vegetables and, according to Alan Waller, who went to see her, "The place was immaculate." At the same time she was also potting, illustrating John's work and bringing up the two children. Each with an energy and focus that made people admire her.

Her potting was becoming more successful and widely sold. Alan Waller remembers visiting her one day only to find he was barred from entering the farm by some men in black suits. His protestations about gaining access had no effect, he simply had to wait outside, which he did. To his amazement, some time later he found the Prince of Wales coming out clutching a whole pile of Sally's pottery.

After a time Sally decided to return to her childhood Australia, settling in northern New

South Wales in 1988. Not only did she start another smallholding but she built the whole farm, house and all, with her own hands. She helped prepare the bricks by making mud. Itinerant brick makers travelled the outback making mud-bricks for homesteaders, and together they produced the raw materials for her new home.

She, with her children, made a life in Australia. She potted and farmed and her days were marked by vigour and a purposeful focus. The difference in her after the stroke was striking, but the smile on her lips, the constantly engaging eyes and a real alertness leads one to believe she will not be beaten by her current problems.

oOo

It is Sunday morning; breakfast is finished - organic bacon and eggs, lots of tea and conversation. Early May warmth streams through the open kitchen door at David and Anne's farmhouse on John and Sally's former Welsh farmland. John and Sally's grandson, Owen, does not follow in his grandfather's footsteps because he loves and talks rugby, which John disliked. Owen, a prop forward, talks of "Big Hits", rucks and mauls, training and the coming season. Sally has eaten and watches our conversation, laughing at the various macho bits which dominate the talk whenever two prop forwards get together.

Sally returns to her room for some time alone and spends the warm May morning looking at woodpeckers attacking the nuts in the hanging bird feeder. She was appalled that Anne did not know what a woodpecker was, something that caused all of us great amusement and good belly laughs accompanied a "what's that bird' competition. After a while Anne got out her boxes of photographs, some of which were of the funeral. It was something of a privilege to be allowed access to these images. They showed people who had only before been names or voices on the telephone, or worse still, signatures on an e-mail. Then we saw John; not John really, merely his shell. It was a little odd at first, looking at John's dead body, but we were kindly brought in to the family and it was not the intrusion we first felt it to be. We had been afforded a privilege that even Sally had not received, because since she had been ill, she had had no chance to view the funeral photographs herself.

Certainly without malice we had been given precedence we did not deserve, and when this fact was realised Sally was invited to join in, being wheeled in to the kitchen. There was no reason to feel uncomfortable, but when Sally saw John dead for the first time she broke down. It was grief too private for us to share and we left to loving smiles and not a few tears. We had only been there for twenty hours, had been admitted as strangers but left as one of them.

Chapter Twelve
John Seymour on ...

John Seymour on Culture

Culture is the means by which people make life bearable. I am not talking of 'High Opera' or 'Jazz' or anything that might be found in the Sunday papers. Culture is what happens when people make food, milk cows, drink beer, fall in love, bury their dead. At least that is the kind of culture John was interested in. Indeed, without this description it would be impossible to really explain what John thought on any subject.

John was a lover of a type of culture that is

characterised by honest-to-goodness ordinary folk, and was impressed not by the pretentious but by the commonplace. Particularly when simple people actually achieve greatness by being ordinary. For example, he writes in his book *About Pembrokeshire* of the people around Whitechurch in the seventeenth century who played chess. Even the most illiterate farmhand could play, and more than one or two great chess men came from the area. Moreover they called the pieces on the chessboard not by their normal names, rook or knight or bishop etc., but by the names of King Arthur's knights.

When he and Sally and the children moved to Wales John assimilated the new culture just as easily as he took to the Irish some years later. Both times there was a shock. He found himself surprised to be living in a peasant economy in Pembrokeshire, was as astonished to be visited by a whole truckload of singing Welshmen to help them harvest grass just as much as he was to find a combine harvesting his wheat in Ireland. Once any rather thin ice had been broken, John was as much a Welshman as he was an Englishman or later just as much an Irishman as he was a Welshman.

John's assimilation of culture is seen in the way he responds to Gypsies. Commissioned by the BBC to do an in-depth study of Gypsies, he already had a head start. He had a long term friendship with Gordon Sylvester Boswell, whom he referred to as Uncle Gordon as a mark of respect. Out of this friendship came a series for radio, a film called *Where do we go from here?*, and possibly, most long lasting a book, *The book of Boswell: The life of a Gypsy Man*. He confessed to a sense of wonder when as a child walking with his nanny, they came across a Gypsy camp. He said that he yearned to go off with them and thought them terribly romantic. To play the 'town councillor attitude' and drive them away because they were different to the rest of us, or to make them conform to our ways was seen by John as a terrible thing. He claimed that it was not the view of many a true countryman either. Gypsies, he believed, were different and therefore interesting, and so should deserve our tolerance. They knew how to live on the road, and they did this by an expression of their culture. They had ways that allowed them to live, knowledge we all need in the world.

He was not too hot on comparing culture. Not believing that one was intrinsically better than another, John answered the charge that Gypsies made a mess of the place with "Yes - but look at the mess we make! Their mess is much more transitory than ours - at least they don't pollute the air and the waters and throw up great factories." He, and the gypsies who welcomed him into their vans, were quick to point out that real gypsies did not steal, or mess up the countryside, wreck parks and terrorise. This was a different people altogether, one that was as despised by true gypsies as everyone else for their antics, the blame for which often fell on them.

Of course, people were his life study, not farming or the countryside. He spent hours and hours working with, and learning the ways of African bushmen when in reality he could have passed his time like so many white men have in Africa; being colonial and giving his orders and having nothing to do with the locals. On his travels overland to India he fell in with so many individuals and families and had numerous encounters and adventures off his actual route, simply because he had the happy knack of making himself attractive to people, learning and mimicking their ways and becoming one of them.

He had plans to start a non-organisation called the Knights of Gaia, individuals dedicated to saving the world, or at least their own part of it. He borrowed the culture of the crusades. Sadly the name has been taken up by a new age board game where children and adults battle together with models of knights and farmers. John's idea was to bring together people who would stand up for 'life' in their areas. There would be no organisation but there would be a newsletter and he clearly planned an international audience. One was to become a Knight of Gaia by reciting an oath in front of at least one other person:

"I declare that all life is sacred. I vow to dedicate

my own life henceforth to defending, cherishing and pro-tecting life on Earth. I hereby declare war on all enemies of life on Earth and I hereby vow to conduct an unremit-ting fight against them. I will behave with true knightly courtesy to all my sister and brother Knights and give them what aid and succour they need."

Incidentally, at the same time that John was work-ing this out an American, Chad Blevins, set up the Knights of Gaia Academy for Conservation and Peace, run on similar lines. They now have a school where people can learn self-sufficiency. The whole point of this non-organisation was that it had its roots in culture. John knew that you could-n't just "stop the planet and get off", people need a cultural backdrop in which to change in relation to others. I once had the opportunity to ask David Bellamy what the hope for the planet was. He said there was none because ordinary people did not care, they were too busy jetting off on holiday three times a year, buying cars, living unsustain-ably. The only way to change these people was to make it culturally acceptable for them to change in the first place. The Knights of Gaia did not take off, possibly because the culture wasn't right.

John celebrated cultures, especially those earthy cultures who live from the land. In particu-lar the Anglo Saxon tendency to record their lives

in story and song impressed him. He said that real
folk songs were always about real people and real
events whereas the American influenced pop song
was almost always about concepts such as love -
not real subjects at all. In 1960 John travelled all
over the country looking for farm people to record
on tape for the BBC. Mr. Arthur Lane, born in
1880, was one of his subjects. Full of his eighty
years, he had been scything grass on a steep hillside
as John drove past. Soon they were drinking home
made wine in Arthur's cottage and he struck up a
song. He was known as Lane the Drum, and he
used to run his Shropshire smallholding behind
Wenlock Edge and sing in the local pub. "Oh, I
used to like to sing and play, days gone by." Arthur continued.
"They always wanted me to go down to the pub -
sing and play to 'em. Don't go there much now
though. But I still love a song."

When six o'clock comes to breakfast we meet
With bread beef and pork boys we'll heartily eat
With a piece in our pocket I'll swear and I'll vow
That we're all jolly fellows that follow the plough!

Working the land was certainly not a sober affair.
It had to be fun, and singing was an integral part of
making life fun. The courses at his home in Wales

and later in Ireland were typically set aside for work and learning during the daytime, but the night time was for playing, story telling, singing, dancing and, of course, drinking. He learned many dozens of songs by heart and his friend and co-author of *Blueprint for a Small Planet*, Herbert Giradet, author and environmental campaigner, said it was because he did not clutter his head up with television programmes.

His trip to Ireland was an eye opener. On the boat over from Wales to Ireland, in the middle of the night in a crowded bar filled with working class Irish men and women, he was treated to a spontaneous concert of folk singing and dancing, Of this spontaneous expression of their cultural roots John wrote,

" *Whether it was the sight of these mountains, or the splendid dawn over the sea, or the wild music that was still ringing in my ears - or all those pints of Guinness I had drunk (and so few of which I had paid for because my friends below had been persistently generous) - I do not know, but I knew that I was going to love this country I was going to. I had fallen head over heels in love with it before I had even set foot upon it.* "

Ireland is just like any other lump of rock sticking

out of the sea, and Ireland would be nothing without the Irish people and their culture, and for John, the same goes for everywhere else on the planet.

John Seymour on Animal Welfare

John killed animals for food. He killed his own chickens, he killed his own pigs, butchered them and preserved their meat. He shot animals in the African bush and on his farms. He fished the seas and the rivers. John was not a vegetarian. Even though he had lived among vegetarians for some time, he didn't choose it as a lifestyle. This is particularly interesting as there were many pressures to be trendy and become a vegetarian when he was running the Centre for Living, but he resisted them. Indeed, a fundamental part of his courses in Wales and Ireland included the killing of animals.

John pointed out that you can eat meat all your life simply by buying it from the butchers and be remote from the actual killing and butchering. But when you kill an animal for yourself the whole matter takes on a completely different perspective. In this matter, self-sufficiency is about taking responsibility for what you put on the table, and in caring for the welfare of any animal and its produce. John saw killing an animal for food as a noble process. I think that John would be the first to agree that the animal itself might have something to say on the matter if it had the chance.

John was an advocate of killing a large animal with a gun rather than a humane killer. The difference as John saw it was that the humane killer had to be held against the animal's head. Sometimes it would co-operate, at other times it would get spooked, and this increased the animal's stress. By using a gun the animal could be despatched with no undue stress at all. Aiming at professionalism in these matters was a case of knowing what was best for the animal. But then we have to obey the law, laws that John said were invented by a town person.

John did not like transporting animals as it made them sick from stress and he was completely against long distance movement of livestock. The journey from the farm to the abattoir was too far for John. He considered the people who protested about the transporting of sheep from the UK to Spain to be heroic in their attempts to gain some rights for these desperate animals. One of the reasons for killing an animal at home was to reduce the stress to the animal. He frequently grew his pigs until they were huge, much bigger than we tend to send them to be despatched these days. This would allow a longer life for the animal and more meat for the human, making it a longer time before another pig should need to be killed.

John was against anything that took away an animal's innate nobility. Crating calves for veal, caging hens in batteries, mass produced pork where the animal is filled with chemicals and kept warm were all high on John's hit list. For John the whole process of living on the planet was an exploration of relationships; man with man, man with animal, man with soil. Anything that threatened that relationship, or exploited the weak for profit, or disregarded the soil or dehumanised the farming process was utterly wrong.

John Seymour on Religion

No one who has worked with animals and seen the seasons change and followed the passage of the seed from a tiny speck to a huge plant can do so without an overriding sense of awe. John saw religion as a sense of awe. Adrienne Murphy, one of the Arthurstown Seven, knew him well enough to say in her obituary for John in the Irish Times that he "seemed to believe in a personal non-dogmatic God." In all his writing and dealings with people the evidence of this all forgiving, all understanding God is seen.

But John had problems with God. He found himself unable to live what might be called a saintly life. The mountain near his Pembrokeshire home was called Carn Ingli. It was a favourite praying place of a Welsh saint, Brynach, and it was said that up the mountain, angels fed him. John complained, "They never fed me, but then I am not a saint." But this did not mean that John was not a spiritual man. He strongly believed in a personal God. More than this, in the world of self-sufficiency as applied to green issues, he believed that we would get nothing right unless we managed to get our spiritual values right.

Coming from a generation who actually believe in nothing has meant that nothing actually matters to them. The result is that western mankind no longer feels that he belongs to Nature, does not feel himself a part of Nature, but that nature (notice the lack of capitalisation) was something to be exploited and plundered. For John, the sooner we find ourselves to be a real part of Nature the better, and this was the whole point and desire of God. The usefulness of any religious experience could be measured, according to John, in how much it encourages this union with Nature. Thus, he argues, Protestantism was the necessary first stage towards the abandonment of all traditional religion because the Reformation that created it was necessary to clear the way for the kind of empirical science that has allowed man to think himself as being separate from Nature.

"If the Europeans had stuck to their Catholic Christian traditions there would have been no Age of Reason - no Industrial Revolution - no Technological Revolution - no

atom bomb - no Windscale - no Three Mile Island or Chernobyl either."

I am sure his pen was firmly in his cheek when he wrote these words in *The Ultimate Heresy*, but the argument does have some logic to it. What he was sure about was that God, by whatever name, was interested in mankind finding himself a part of Nature, and having got this right, all the rest would follow. His argument is somewhat similar to C S Lewis' in *Out of the Silent Planet*. The Earth is out of kilter caused by man's separation from the basic principles of Life akin to Wordsworth's "Our birth is but a sleep and a forgetting..."

John admitted to praying. *"Not like Maggie Thatcher on top of the atom pile - I stand, out of doors, with my head high, and fling my arms out wide and open to embrace, ritually, all the matter of the Universe, animate and inanimate."*

He did not think it important to chase around the world following other religions. He believed there was a religious enlightenment available to communities which was both historically and culturally correct. He thought it important to 'make something' of the religion that *belonged* to an area. This was with the aim of bringing man to firmly believe he was a part of Nature, where he would not dream of hunting to extinction or poison the water or the air: This, he thought, was the very essence of all religion. For John, this was evangelism worthy of the name. He found uses for all religious experience. He read and quoted the Bhagavad Gita, and found this quite compatible with kneeling at the Blessed Sacrament, which he did as a part of his community in Co. Wexford, Ireland. Why should a Buddhist in India want to become a Roman Catholic like those in Italy? It wouldn't offer them any more enlightenment, and would be culturally out of place.

On his travels whilst in the Army through Ceylon, John came into close contact with Asian culture for the first time. He was completely bowled over by it, and started to examine ancient Hinduism. He believed that much of the thought behind all religions had already been expressed by these people, and thus he was led to re-examine Christianity. He read the Bible in a new light and he said that this knowledge did not make him believe more fully in the doctrines of his mother religion, but they did awaken in him a deeper interest, more ready to go deeper than a mere superficial rejection for its own sake. In later life John more fully embraced Roman Catholicism, attended Mass and did his best to incorporate the teachings of this brand of Christianity into his daily life. His version of Catholicism was greatly coloured by the culture of the people he learned it from - the people of Co. Wexford.

Whether it was initiated by the state of the planet, pollution, atomic power, nuclear weapons, or whether it was some doctrinal motivation, John had an apocalyptic vision of the world. A battle between good and evil that was one between the Life Force, or God if you like, and those others opposed to life on the planet. He said that, as described in the book of Genesis, man and woman were placed on the planet to tend the garden, and that God's ultimate ideal for man was to live in a garden - a planet sized garden.

John Seymour on the Politics of the Land

John was drinking with a bunch of soldiers in an Irish Pub. They were singing the old songs of rebellion and generally having a good time when they noticed he was English. "How can you join in with these anti-English songs?" His reply took them aback a little. "I am an Englishman, and you are singing about what the English government did to you three hundred years ago. I would remind you that the same government was doing much the same to its own working people as it was to your ancestors." The Irish peasantry were not, in John's view, the enemies of the English peasantry. And so, if they didn't mind, he would get drunk with them, eat with them and sing their songs of rebellion.

John documented the removal of the peasantry from the land many times. He saw it as an

important thing to do since without peasants own-
ing and caring for the land it would naturally fall
into disrepair, for who would do their best for a
land that they didn't own? Following the Black
Death of 1348 - 49 farming in Britain changed.
Previously peasants paid for their land by service,
which meant a day a week on the whole, working
for the manor. After the plague they started to demand money and could get high wages, but then
they had to pay money back in rent for their own
lands and homes. John argued that this land should
have remained in the actual ownership of the peasants because it was their ancestors who "hacked it
out of the forest, and their ancestors and themselves who had done all the hard work since to
keep it that way."

Shortly after this the 'sheep boom' made English wool so sought after that landowners found
they could make much more money from sheep
than from any other method of farming. They
fenced off the common land and the open fields
and in many cases threw the people out of their
homes and burned the houses down. Sheep only
needed a few shepherds to look after them and
whole communities died. John wrote in *The Countryside Explained*, of some of the uprisings of the
peasantry at this time. One such was led by Robert
Kett of Norfolk. He had been a landowner himself,
enclosing many fields before changing his mind and
returning the land to his tenants. He led a revolt

that took all of Norfolk and Suffolk and captured Norwich. When he was defeated, by an army of German mercenaries, they slaughtered so many peasants that it was reported that the Earl of Warwick, the King's leader in these matters, asked "Is there no place for pardon? Shall we hold the plough ourselves, and harrow our own lands?"

The peasants were largely driven from the land and ended up in expanding towns. A revolution was about to take place that John thought was the basis of good farming. Enclosures eventually made it possible for families to own parcels of land, build their own home on their own land and be responsible for it. This way a family might be able to intimately know their own land, nurture its fertility, even love it. This relationship with the land should be, in John's view, the basis for good and healthy families, a stable rural economy, an environment not plagued by excessive use of pesticides or oil based fertilisers. Ownership of the land is such an important factor in producing a healthy agriculture.

Compare this situation to that in Ireland where people were kept separate from the ownership of the land. They had to rent it, and rent can be used as a political force either for good as with the peppercorn rent, or for bad such as the rackrent already discussed that took place in Ireland. Catholic peasants were charged a huge proportion of their income as rent and should they not be able to pay, they were evicted - literally thrown out of their homes. The reason why potatoes were grown more than any other crop was because they could be left in the ground. Grain crops had to be harvested and stored. It was much easier for the land owners to take the whole crop - but they would not dig up potatoes to collect a debt.

People kept pigs and poultry but never tasted their meat or eggs because they were too expensive and were being reared simply to cover the rent. The land was in full supply, yet people starved, indeed they were starving well before the potato famine decimated the population of Ireland. Thackery. the nineteenth century writer, toured Ireland and reported on the state of the starving people. He wrote of a tract of land that had previously been swamp and had been settled by Irish colonists who drained the pasture, built homes and set up their enclosures. It was '... land that had not since the Deluge fed any being bigger than a snipe, and into which the poor had descended ..." There were now two hundred homesteads where as many families lived in comfort and plenty."

This was John's material point, and there is no better way of putting it than in his own words. " *If you give a family its fair share of the earth's surface and leave it in peace, the members of that family will soon find a way of living 'in comfort and plenty' if they are any good at all.*"

Land reform was a necessary part of his grand plan to save the earth from agri-businessmen who would pollute the land, who would take small units and make enormous ones, who would dream up things such as genetically modified organisms.

Although John had people staying with him on a regular basis, and ran a school of self-sufficiency, he never actually believed in the commune. It did seem to visitors at times that his farm appeared to be a bit that way, but the people staying with them were either friends or learning how to farm. Actual ownership of the land and family ties were for John the most important motivations for making sure that the farm was husbanded properly. This is one of the reasons why they left their place in Suffolk and moved to Pembrokeshire, so they could actually own the land they were improving.

Governments, John pointed out, had the wrong end of the stick in their mandate to make farmers richer. Short of increasing the land available for farming, or the actual cost of food, the only other way to make *some* farmers richer was to make their farms bigger. This seems to have taken place in the UK. Small farms have gone to the wall, but at the same time, large farms have become larger. The displaced people from farming now live in the cities, and this has presented two problems in order to be able to feed them. Firstly conventional farming has had to produce food in a

non-sustainable way, using the oil economy to
back it up in terms of energy, fertilisers and pesticides. Secondly, since we do not produce enough
food in this country for everyone, and pretty much
the same can be said for every 'Western' nation,
then the globalisation of food supplies has had to
take place. The market garden, the old geographi-
cal concept of the hinterland, food producers selling through supermarkets, is now no longer a few
miles outside the city, but thousands of miles
away, all around the world. Simple ownership of
small farms by small farmers (economically speaking) is John's answer to these problems, but to
achieve this would imply an enormous change in
the way we live, and here the real problems come
to the surface. An exodus of people from the cities
to the land is in many ways already under way.
Those who can afford it sell their homes and buy a
little piece of countryside. A recent newspaper
report said there were five million families thinking seriously of giving up the rat race, avoiding urban crime and deteriorating living standards, and
looking to the rural idyll for escape. They are at
present mostly keeping ponies, but eventually,
John argued, they will have to actually live off the
land they own. In order to do this they will need
to revive the skills half lost by misuse of living in
the countryside, as they can no longer rely on
supermarkets to help them with their daily bread.

It was John's life work to provide some of

these skills, carefully recorded and accessible to all.

John Seymour on Distributism

John's later life attachment to Roman Catholicism can be explained in terms of Distributism. It was propounded in the nineteenth century and later, by a number of leading thinkers including Pope Leo XII, G. K. Chesterton, Hilaire Belloc, and Dorothy Day. Basically it encapsulates the idea that the land, and the means of the production from the land, should be owned by as many people as is possible. A seminal work by Pope Leo XIII in 1891 called *Rerum Novarum reads:*

"If working people can be encouraged to look forward to obtaining a share in the land, the consequence will be that the gulf between vast wealth and sheer poverty will be bridged over, and the respective classes will be brought nearer to one another. A further consequence will result in the greater abundance of the fruits of the earth. Men always work harder and more readily when they work on that which belongs to them, nay, they learn to love the very soil that yields in response to the labour of their hands, not only food to eat, but an abundance of good things for themselves and those that are dear to them. That such a spirit of willing labour would add to the produce of the earth and to the wealth of the community is self-evident. And a third advantage would spring

*from this: men would cling to the country in which they
were born; for no one would exchange his country for a
foreign land if his own afforded him the means of living
a decent and happy life. . ."*

You can see that John would have few problems
saying "Amen' to that. The roots of Distributism
were fashioned in a theory by G. K. Chesterton
and Hilaire Belloc in the first decade of the twentieth century. It was an ongoing conversation that
became known as the 'the Chesterbelloc Contro-
versy'. John himself said that he didn't know he
was a Distributist until he read Belloc and his
books became a close companion for many years.
The Servile State by Belloc, written before John was
born, was an important force in the promotion of
the ideas that John later espoused. Belloc wrote
that if you have to pay taxes on property you actually do not own that property but merely lease it
from the government. John himself said that if you
rent a man a piece of land he will wreck it, but if
you give him a piece of land he will make it into a
productive paradise.

Belloc was a man whose pen was always at
work. A man of opinions and an easy target for
mud-slingers, a life led in many ways resembling
John's own. The theory of Distributism led to the
'back to the land' movements in the United States,
and, largely due to John's influence, here in the
United Kingdom. Many economists would look at

distributism as a dead force, a quaint idea that never got anywhere, but if they were to look more closely they would find thousands of families actually living the life or aiming to live the life that encompasses Belloc and Chesterton's ideas.

John Seymour on the nuclear age

John fought his way through Africa, India and into Burma. He fought against Germans, Italians and Japanese, and admitted that he killed many. He was certainly no pacifist. When he heard of the atomic bomb attack on Hiroshima on August 6th 1945, and later on Nagasaki on the 9th of August, he said it was a cowardly thing to do. He said that because of this he was ashamed to fight for the allies. He called the weapons themselves megadeaths. This was a corruption of the word megaton, equating the power of an atomic device in millions of tonnes of TNT. He campaigned against nuclear weapons, considering them unmanly as much as immoral. Some lines from The Nuclear Physicist's Alphabet show his point of view.

A is for the Atom we all love to split
B's for the bombs that we make out of it
C's for Chernobyl we try to forget
And D's for the Doomster who's nothing but a wet.

One gets the distinct impression of John banging his head against a brick wall. While in Ireland he was involved in a number of campaigns as a Patron of many green groups aimed at the Sellafield atomic facility in the English Lake District. Previously known as Windscale, but changed to Sellafield following an almost disastrous accident where it had been leaking radioactive material over the local countryside. It also became known as "the sieve" for obvious reasons. The Irish government and a large number of individuals had been campaigning against nuclear discharges into the Irish Sea and John added his voice to them. Paddy Mackey, a founder of VOICE, the organisation that replaced Greenpeace Ireland, remembers John being somewhat disappointed with them because he thought they were not doing enough. John said, at the end of a particularly heavy drinking session in Dublin, that he "... *wanted to blow something up to make them sit up and take notice.*" Through this group he became involved in Greenpeace International and was vocal against all forms of nuclear experimentation for peace or war. He believed that there was enough energy in the world, we just had to learn how to tap into it in a clean fashion.

On the other hand John did not believe we actually needed all that energy in the first place. By living frugally there would be no energy shortage. Burning wood in a renewable way was the age old method of keeping warm and cooking in a sustainable way, growing that which had been burned collecting as much greenhouse gasses as it gave off. He had been using windmills since his first days in Africa, when his life, and the lives of his stock, depended on the water they drew from the rocks hundreds of feet below the earth. Students at The Centre for Living learned how to build windmills and solar panels as well as milk cows and till the earth.

John Seymour on agri-business

A demure Indian lady, Dr Vandana Shiva, speaks with a laugh in her voice and a smile on her face. Her friendliness hides a strong woman who fights tooth and nail for the rights of the small farmer. Her smiling voice came through on a crackling telephone line one day, "They want to reduce the number of farmers on the planet from a few billion to just four!" She has taken on the large agri-businessmen in the courts of India and won, but it is only a cosmetic victory. The true centre of warfare for the small farmer is in the lobby of the bank. Peasant Indian farmers are being encouraged to grow unsuitable genetically modified crops and use unsustainable amounts of pesticide and fertiliser. At the same time the cost of food in the shops, she alleged, is being kept unfairly low by using the subsidies of the World Bank and the

International Monetary Fund that should be going to farmers but is actually going to shopkeepers. The result is that farmers cannot sell their crops and eventually they loose their farms to the bank. Culturally there is great loss of face and implied shame for the farmer, and Shiva says thousands have killed themselves by drinking weed killer as a result. The land is snapped up by agri-business to be turned into larger units which, by their size and financial backing, are then portrayed as the future of modern farming.

Vandana Shiva was a close friend, conference speaker colleague and ally of John Seymour. He constantly abhorred the process of manipulation of the marketplace to the detriment of the small farmer that has been going on in the UK for years. John was a proponent of what his friend, Professor Leopold Kohr, coined as 'small is beautiful', a concept popularised by their mutual friend, Fritz Schumacher in his book of the same name. The concept of small is beautiful, of course, can be applied to farms. The small farm is owned by the small farmer. He cares for the land, he has a relationship with the land which John called husbandry, and the life of the farmer and the land he farms is mutually dependant.

Huge fields of hundreds of acres of monocrop, owned by a man in an office in a different city, or even a different continent, where what happens to the actual soil is dictated not by what it needs or what the farmer needs, but by minute changes in the cost of chemicals, the price of oil, exchange rates or war in some far off corner of the world, made John sick. The other side of agri-business, the oil based high input, high poison, high fertiliser, saviour of the chemical industry side of agri-business was also the recipient of John's campaigning. He was literally hated by Monsanto's board of Directors, for one of whom John wrote a rhetorical poem.

John's plan for the fertility of a farm relied on a cow. This animal was the basis of a healthy family. It provided milk and meat and when the milk finally ran out, it provided replacement cows and, more than anything, it provided manure. One cow, half a dozen pigs and a few hens would provide enough fertiliser to keep five acres perfectly fertile. John's plan for fertility was taken quite literally when groups like the Catholic Aid Agency, CAFOD, started to donate cattle from the west to African villages, not just for the milk they provide, but for the fertility they put into the soil.

As we have already seen, John became famous for the stance he took with many others against a Monsanto test crop of genetically modified (GM) sugar beet. He was outspoken, along with many others, against what he called genetically mutilated plants. He pointed out that there were many reasons for opposing GM crops. Sure, there was the possibility that the genes could infect other crops, but there were more important and pressing problems. Firstly, GM was not for the good of the world, but the good of the companies that created and sold the seed. He simply could not bring himself to trust rich businessmen with the precious nature of living off the land; he already knew how they thought because of the way his step father thought. In order to monopolise their investment the law was used that said a company had copyright over a particular combination of genes, and that the use of plants bearing this combination of genes is prohibited to the sole discretion of the copyright holder. In other words, people could neither save seed to sow the following year, or sell the seed or develop crops suitable for certain environments from the seed. This is the most important point, in John's view.

In India the micro-climate of various regions has meant that dozens of different varieties of wheat have been produced to suit the dynamics of the areas they are grown in. One variety grows well in one place, and another somewhere else. Wheat from India fed much of the British Empire in the early years of the twentieth century. The 'men in white coats' as John called them have recently tried to replace them by a single GM variety. If they were really biologists they would understand that a single crop was bound to fail in many places. Nature favours diversity. The production of new varieties should be in the control of the people that are growing the crop themselves. Take away their right to do so and you steal from them. John, Vandana Shiva and many, many others considered this to be the greatest evil of the modern world.

John Seymour on Supermarkets

John pledged not to enter a supermarket in the 1960s when he was living at Broom. He seemed to develop this side of his thinking very early on as the stranglehold of the domestic market was only just beginning. In this way his ideas were far reaching and before their time. Living in the country, miles from anywhere, he could hardly have come across one, and the supermarkets of the time would be considered small by today's standards. However, his feelings were proven to be right and what he predicted has come to pass.

1950s Britain boasted hundreds of thousands of independent shopkeepers supplying the lion's share of the food. Fifty years later the vast majority of the food we eat today is sold by only four or five companies. People collect their food from faceless shelves, collated by computers, filled by people on the minimum wage. Computers open and close the doors for you, they work out which shelves need filling and order the replacements, they cut and pack meat and cheese, the milk we drink, even the vegetables are farmed to order by computers from all over the world. Food is frequently cooked by computer and all we need is a computer telling us the best time to eat it and thus our removal from the world of food will be complete. But then many of us *are* called to eat by computers!

John believed that to take the human element out of any process that affects our lives was a mean thing to do. Supermarkets for him were mean places, where it was possible to buy food, but not to enjoy the getting of food. Even someone who did not grow or produce any of their own food could enjoy a social event every time they went shopping, talking to perhaps a dozen or more shopkeepers in the process. Now it was possible to do a weekly shop without having to talk to anyone, and this was a terrible loss for humanity, social structure and cultural cohesion.

What is more, shopping was to be done by car, miles away from where you lived and this would have an isolating effect on people. Coming out of the house, getting into the car, driving to the shop, returning with bags of shopping and dragging it back into the house takes all the interaction with people out of daily life. Conversation with non-family members is frequently confined to discussing the holidays with a taxi driver. This modern way of life was certainly anathema to John Seymour. He predicted that it would lead to a disintegration of society.

Importantly, John foresaw a time when the very nature of farming and food production would change because of supermarkets. Because they controlled the markets it would be possible for them to control what was suitable for those markets. Ordinary food such as amusingly shaped carrots, turnips with a bit of dirt on them, eggs with chicken 'poo' on them would no longer be allowed in the shops. As John described, everything now has to be grown to an exacting standard which frequently means that perfectly good food that would have been acceptable in the past cannot be grown. Moreover, the cost to the supermarket, the timing of the delivery and costs involved in producing the 'perfect' product have influenced a certain type of farming; one that produces bigger farms with more mechanisation, more oil and fewer people to the detriment of rural communities.

Politically, consumerism is changing the world. This is fuelled in no small measure by supermarkets sourcing internationally. It is not uncommon to see seven or eight varieties of tomato, or lettuce, or potato on supermarket shelves, each one grown in a different part of the world. There will be a local variety, one from Spain, another from South America, South Africa and so on. Transportation costs assimilated into the purchase price do not take into account that there are additional hidden costs that are borne by the planet, in greenhouse gas and pollution and in human costs.

John was always quick to spot these human costs. There are farmers in South America growing crops for British, European and American markets, and probably more, but who is growing crops for them? In the end, someone is having to grow food with nothing left for themselves. The system will always have a large number of losers and this kind of consumerism is simply an extension to the 'rack renting' that John complained of in Ireland because it results in people growing food they cannot afford to eat themselves.

John Seymour on Racism

Maybe this section should have been put next to the one on culture, since diversity of culture is partially racial. But in another way it deserves to be separate because it is good to avoid cultural clash and all that this implies. John was not, when in Africa, trying to force a white European way of life on the African native. Similarly, on his travels through Asia and India he never actually thought his upbringing or his way of life to be any better than anyone else's. Indeed, he frequently realised that the ordinary native, uneducated and illiterate though he may have been judged and measured in western terms, was very bright and intelligent, probably more so than your average white person.

He did not believe in the 'boss and kafir' society that he found in Africa. He did believe in people, whether they were white or black. He called the system of apartheid a sick distortion of humanity, and he recognised that the black man had been dispossessed from the land more utterly in Africa than anywhere else. This was in part due to the fact that wherever you went you could, if you were a white man, press any black man into service, have them arrested, beaten or even killed.

John bucked the system wherever he could. He went out on clandestine hunting missions with natives and placed himself in the position of pupil to their superior knowledge. He was unable to relate to fellow white men, frequently officers in the army, because of their attitude. However, John believed there was a place for the European in Africa. They brought ways of improving agriculture in places. He also thought that that natives often had ancient ways of living that were not suited to the complete change that had come about in their country. He said that various groups lived a stone age existence, but did not for one moment imply that modern man was any better. He was vociferous in their defence when the state or farmers or the police perpetrated injustices against them.

The John Seymour Manifesto

When his eyesight was failing and his health looking as though it would not simply recover as it always had in the past, John wrote an article for *Resurgence* magazine. He was proud of this connec-
tion, and grateful for the opportunity to present to
a wide public some theoretical aspects of his thinking and way of life. His theoretical writings were
actually very practical in their foundation. He
nearly always wrote from his direct experience and
the accumulation of this was poured into a piece
called *The Age of Healing*.

In it he argued that the Age of Enlightenment, a time of great change in Europe in regard
to science, the arts and politics and described by
John as the time when man thought he knew better
than God, was naturally followed by an Age of
Plunder. This time has been marked by greed in
such voracity to make the planet sick. John said
that the Age of Plunder was coming to an end because the world system, the 'Thing' as Cobbett described it, was too large and unwieldy. Moreover,
the pollution and devastation of the Age of Plunder
was about to destroy its activities anyway. John
saw two scenarios that might mark an end to the
Age of Plunder; one being the Age of Chaos, the
other being the Age of Healing.

How was the Age of healing to be brought

about? True to his 'small is beautiful' roots, John
suggested that it could be done by individuals.
Reminiscent of his Knights of Gaia of some years
previous, he suggested a motto, an oath by which
people could pledge themselves to help bring in an
Age of Healing.

> " *I am only one.*
>
> *I can only do what one can do.*
>
> *But what one can do I will do!* "

But what was one to do? Was one to 'blow something up' as John confessed he wanted to do in his
more youthful early eighties, or get arrested for
uprooting GM crops? Like all revolutions that last,
John's plan was simple, and easily understood:

Refuse to work for the plunderers

Anything that made the greedy richer would only
encourage them. Refusing to labour for them
would not only stop 'the Thing' from getting bigger, it would make you a better person. John believed in the link between ownership and labour.
Working all day on something that belonged to
someone else to receive only enough payment to
force you to have to turn up the following day to
do the same is a form of slavery that most of us
cannot avoid. If you can find work that benefits

you and your family and no one else you will be better at it, more content and you won't be contributing to the plunderers.

R efuse to shop in the plunderers' supermarkets

We have already explored reasons for John not going into a supermarket. Apart from directly influencing the plunder of the planet to furnish their shelves, John hinted at the type of goods they sell as 'shoddy', and that we should refuse to buy them. In *The Fat of the Land*, John described factory made items in relation to the people in the factories that made them. Do they live a better life than the average peasant in France? It might be an easier life, but was it better, healthier, more fulfilling? And the products themselves, made by machine, lack that human touch that made them, in John's eyes at least, not worth having.

"*As far as we can we import our needs from small and honest craftsmen and tradesmen. We subscribe as little as we can to the tycoons, and the Ad-men, and the boys with the expense accounts. If we could subscribe nothing at all we would be the better pleased.*"

Give up the desire for large wealth

This means not doing the lottery, not because you would not have won it in the first case, but because you don't want the money anyway. If you want to change your life, John would argue, 'change it!' but don't wait for the lottery to change it for you.

Chances are that you would not win, but if you did it would not actually change you very much. You would remain umbilically attached to the system, its money, its shops and its way of plunder. John argued that people who desire to live like a Texan millionaire and take on credit and live unsustainable lives were killing the planet.

Endure financial hardship

People should withhold work and investment from plundering industries. This would inevitably hurt us financially, but this should be endured for the good of everyone. You really have to believe to be able stick to this, because financial hardship for the sake of coming out of the system is not culturally accepted. A change in culture would help, perhaps we could get together and create a culture where people shared their burdens in an out of the system way that was ordinary, not weird of hippy-like, just plain ordinary?

Work, always, for a decentralist economy

If everything you acquire and the services you use come from far away, planned by someone in another city, or country, how can your local community maintain itself? All the decisions about it are out of the hands of locals. Everything, from waste collection to policing, becomes big business and considerations of economy outweigh quality. For instance, responsibility for school meals was taken out of the hands of individual schools and taken over by Education Authorities. In turn, this was sub-contracted to companies who, as a business and not a service, catered for schools in a number of authority areas. The result was that pot plates and bowls were replaced by plastic mess trays and children only had about 12% of the cost of the meal spent on actual food. Parents had no choice in this process, and many children voted with their feet, bringing sandwiches. But the vulnerable children, those on free school meals, ended up with much less nourishment than they would have had under the old system.

Take part in your local politics

Boycott the politics of the huge scale, the remote and the far-away. He was virulently against the

EU. Indeed he argued frequently for an independent Wales, Scotland and Northern Ireland. John's ideas on the sanctity of human life made it an imperative that campaigns should be non-violent. He cited the non-violent defiance of the law by people protesting against the export of live animals from Britain as a fine example of citizen-power. He always said that if the EU were ever to try to tax him, he would not pay it.

Fair shares for all

Not Communism but Distributism. John believed that we should work for a system where the land was shared out equally between all the people. Certainly they should buy their plot of land, and planning laws should be changed to allow them to live off it. This would eliminate poverty among those who were willing to work for the well being of their families and at the same time release a surplus for those who needed it. The whole point is that people would have enough, but not too much, and that is all they would want. Why should anyone want more? This state of mind has educational and cultural implications.

Oppose new road building

John saw that road transport was choking the

atmosphere and a major contribution to pollution problems globally. People living in cities need not use a car at all, it being cheaper and healthier to use other forms of transport. People living in the country might need a car, but they should use it sparingly. Of course, the cost of car hire was much better than car ownership. Sourcing goods with the fewest road miles and for that matter air miles was the best way to reduce the need for transport. New roads, John argued, like so many campaigners around Britain, never actually eased traffic congestion, but made it worse. The only way to solve traffic problems was to reduce the amount of traffic.

Boycott imported culture

Whether by economic or military or political means the domination of one culture over another represented, in John's mind, an invasion. Leaving behind the traditional culture of an endemic people for another culture from a foreign land was not only a betrayal of what had happened in the past, but an unsustainable acceptance of something not particular suited to life in the particular locality. As we have already seem, the village of Blaxhall, where John's favourite pub the Ship is situated, used to be populated with farm workers, farmers and the associated tradesmen to furnish them. The fact that the village is largely populated by teachers, holiday homes, health professionals - almost anything other than farm workers - is due to two things; the change in the farming industry and the acceptance of the people of the village of another way of life. John despised the implication of anyone telling him what to do, and the imposition of culture is just that.

Encourage local credit

Credit Unions have long been a way that the local community could invest in local people. Banks invest their money in the stock exchange, local credit unions invest their money in local people and local industry. The means of getting credit in the first place is only based on the input you have made into the scheme. It is not subject to any other status, and this reflects the means by which people should be able to live. They get credit because they have something in common with the other people in the Credit Union, and they have put into the scheme themselves. Banks invest in risk and charge according to the risk. Credit Unions invest in the people and charge for the benefit of the other people they serve. When Building Societies bought themselves out of their members in the 'carpet bagging' days, they sold, for mere money, a tradition that valued people and their

locality (every town or county had its own building society) for a tradition that values mere profit.

Buy or grow organically

If you buy organic food you will strike a blow
against the agri-business giants who are using oil to
create poisons to control pests and artificial fertilisers to force plants to grow in an unnatural way. If
you boycott all non-organic products then the
companies that produce them will lose money.
Also you will be better, healthier and fitter and
avoid chemicals that promote all kinds of terrible
diseases. I don't know, however, how you could
buy organic produce from the other side of the
world. Especially if the ground they were grown in
was organic because a year ago it was virgin rain
forest or some other natural resource. The
emissions involved in flying a kilo of produce from
the other side of the world turns even the most
organic of products into a dangerously polluting
liability. How can this be organic?

Buy compassionately

Boycott anything you know to have been produced
involving animal cruelty or human exploitation. In
all John's travels when people lived off the land
human culture was proven to be compassionate.

When the big, the corporation, the multi-national business, the vested interest, the 'do for profit' and the greedy are allowed their way, compassion goes out of the window.

John ended his essay with the following words:

The tiny amount you and I can do is hardly likely to bring the huge worldwide moloch of plundering industry down? Well, if you and I don't do it, it will not be done, and the Age of Plunder will terminate in the Age of Chaos. We have to do it - just the two of us - just you and me. There is no " them" - there is nobody else. Just you and me. On our infirm shoulders we must take up this heavy burden now - the task of restoring the health, the wholeness, the beauty and the integrity of our planet. We must start the Age of Healing now!

Tomorrow will be too late.

Chapter Thirteen
Do You Think They Took Him Seriously?

The world out of which John passed is very different than the one into which he was born. Attitudes about what constitutes a happy and worthwhile life have changed, people are no longer willing to settle for the kind of life their great grandparents lived. The toil, the poverty, the exploitation and life expectations of a few generations ago seem to us to be almost prehistoric, never to be returned. But there remain some serious questions about the way we live: plundering both human populations and the planet itself to provide a lifestyle that is unreasonably costly in terms of energy and planetary resources as well as pollution. But is there something more; is there a way to combine the goals of modern people with the needs of the planet? I realise this is a naive question. What is better? What constitutes a happy life? John was interested in capturing the heart of ordinary folk, the folk who now drive big cars in this country, travel abroad, live easily.

The problem with modern society is that we have all become so dependent upon what John, quoting Cobbett, called 'The Thing', that we no longer imagine a society without it. With this in mind John wrote a story for Dara Molloy, a Celtic Monk who lived in a unique community at An Charraig, on the Isle of Arran. He invited John and Angela to speak at what they called a 'conversation on self-sufficiency'. Over the years, Dara and John had various meetings and found they had an affinity for each other. "There is something of the monk in John" Dara said.

The story was of an imaginary island which had little soil, but what there was, was fertile. The people of the island made comfortable lives for themselves. The soil grew richer and more fertile, there was rock for building and reed for thatching. The sea was teeming with fish and the island supported a large and prosperous society.

There were some important commodities the islanders needed to import; wood, fuel, a teacher for the children, but these they paid for with sheep, cattle and fish. There was no need for anyone to go hungry or without homes so long as they were not too lazy to work for them. When the population became too large, a few would go to the mainland, but they frequently returned.

A pair of brothers lived on the island and one of them decided to leave, the other stayed. After many years of being successful in the city the brother returned. He had become flabby and unfit but he had money with which he set about changing the island.

He built an airport and hotels and roads. Tourists came in to the area and the locals decided that they too wanted cars - even though their island was tiny. People no longer bothered to go fishing, except for fun, and the farming languished. Those who had grown vegetables and crops ceased to do so, preferring to go to the supermarket on the mainland. People who had cows didn't milk them but bought their milk from the mainland. There was still a little trade in store cattle and fat lamb and all the wool was sent to the mainland where it fetched practically nothing. It became valueless and the people bought all their clothes from mainland shops instead of making their own.

Soon the people of the island were not making anything for themselves but depended totally on tourism for their money, which they spent on the mainland. No one asked the question that might have been obvious: What if the tourists stopped coming? Of course, the whole economy was fuelled by debt. Banks on the mainland funded a building programme. They swapped their homes for bungalows and instead of the exertions of daily toil for food in the field, in the sea, in the sheepfold or milking parlour, making them lean and fit, the exaction of the bank and the 'system' made them fat and worried. They lost the freedom to direct their own lives.

The brother who stayed on the island was in

a bad way; his car was broken, the washing machine was broken and the children were a bigger drain on their finances. He went to bed worried, woke early still worried and worked daily - worried. One night he had a dream. He dreamed of a huge vacuum cleaner sucking money, animals, soil - everything there was - out of the island. He had to hold on to his door post in order to stop the huge vacuum cleaner from taking him too. He realised that the hose was taking the very life from the island and depositing it into the mainland, into the banks and the pockets of millionaires. The realisation woke him up. After a glass of poteen (well it was John that was writing this!) he decided there must be a way forward to take his island out of the trouble in to which they had got themselves. In the story John renamed this brother as The Dreamer. He wrote a plan of action to save the islands.

Firstly, they should set up one man to become a dairy farmer who would have access to all the grass on the island and all would promise to support him. They could make their own butter and cheese and any number of high class dairy products for their own consumption. The capital needed to start this enterprise off was to come solely from themselves, not borrowed from a bank or anyone else. They would use their own Credit Union.

Secondly, they would set up an abattoir and

kill their own animals which they would rear themselves.

Thirdly they would make their own cloth and consequently their own clothes, just as they had done in the past.

Fourthly they would get people to garden again, maybe keep a few hens, even pigs.

Fifthly they would aim at becoming self-sufficient in energy and finally they would ban cars from the island.

So, the Dreamer told the prominent islanders of his plan and did they listen to him? Not a fat chance!

But people do listen. I used to work with an African, Dr Habakkuk Yongo. Habakkuk was a financial adviser to the Nigerian government. At the time Nigeria was just coming out of civil war and the country had a huge debt. Habakkuk, a small man with an infectious laugh, found himself working in the state bank as a business advisor and trouble shooter. He advised the government not to pay the national loans to the IMF and the World Bank but use the money to get the country on its feet and then start to repay the loans when Nigeria was in a stronger financial position. They took his advice and the result? Within six months there was a coup d'Etat. Some general or other, sponsored by some country or other, took over Nigeria. The military government immediately started paying the international loan payments and Dr. Yongo was convinced that the military coup was sponsored by the United States and the United Kingdom. Whether this was actually true or not, the payments to foreign government banks and international monetary institutions restarted and it is possible to be sympathetic with Habakkuk's conclusion.

People, governments, banks and institutions do actually take notice. The problem is that the real people who matter, you and me, tend to prefer the so called better, easier life provided by the 'Thing' and so do not take notice of what is happening under our very noses.

There are plenty of groups, people, governments even, who are crying out that the life we are leading is not sustainable. There are those who are measuring the temperature of ice caps, others the width of the ozone layer, others measuring the pH balance of the rain. We have people building wind turbines for green environmental reasons, others opposing them for the same overall cause. There are those worried about food, pollution, GM, carcinogens in the water supply, the rights of animals, foxes, sheep. The 'green' movement is awash with different people motivated by assorted ideologies from religion to profit.

John was different. You see, his legacy to us is a simple one. It was humanity. I am not trying to make a religious point here, but merely a human one. John was a bloke, a man who liked a drink, a man who loved and had a complex side to his nature, who loved his senses as well as his brain, who lived with and worked alongside other men and saw the whole world in relation to those he loved. He understood poverty because he understood what it was like to owe the bank huge sums of money and he understood what it was like to worry about it. He knew the meaning of liberty because he saw the look on the faces of those to whom he gave liberally of his possessions, and then some more. He knew the deepest reverence owed to even the lowliest South African because they lived off their land in such a way that drew respect from him.

John was the first to put environmental problems in human terms. He was interested in people and his goal was to build healthy societies of people first and foremost. The way we tread lightly on the planet was to love people first, people encouraged to have their own acre, and make a Paradise of it. For John, an Earth without people was unthinkable. He didn't simply relate green politics in relation to human populations or demographics, but in relation to families. Actual real people, in much the same way that he saw real songs as being about factual happenings to real persons. Only when families coveted their own acre or two of land and worked to get it with their own resources, and having got it worked to make profitable use of the land to feed their own children and to love, (yes love) their own soil that gave them life day by day, would there be real hope for a locality. Those who do not choose to take this way, in John's mind, and dare I beg a seat next to him, confine themselves to poverty.

So what actually is poverty? Accountants, governments and banks measure wealth in terms of what they can take off you. Bankers give mortgages in respect to how trustworthy you are and how much you can afford to repay. The more you can afford, the more you can have. But if I buy a farm, say the size of Broom, with a mortgage, I would have to pay well over a million pounds at current prices and the repayments on such a mortgage would be enormous. So much so that I could not live off the land. For the next twenty five years I belong to the bank. Take the family living in an average house anywhere in Britain. They own it, mortgages of course, they have a car, maybe two. They have TV and enough money to buy food and holidays and have a little in the bank. On the internet there is a website where you can put in details of your income and it will calculate how many people are worse off than you. The average person in the United Kingdom is said to have over six billion people less rich than themselves.

Compare this to a subsistence farmer in Africa. He goes hungry, his children receive no education, there is no medical assistance, he scrapes a living from the soil augmented by what he can kill from the bush. He owns land, and his hut. No car, no electric power, few clothes, no riches.

But what if 'The Thing' collapses? Then you are there in a house without power because you cannot afford to pay the bills, and a garden so small that you could not even feed one person. Who is the richer? The only accumulated wealth a European has, in the direst sense, is the fat he has accumulated around his waist, which is killing him now by adding to the stress on his heart, but might keep him alive for a few months should everything else fail. The subsistence farmer would still continue, scratching a living as he and his forebears have for generations.

John's legacy is that real accounting of wealth should be measured on one thing, the ability of humans to live well and prosperously depending only on their own community. A rich person would not be wealthy financially, but wealthy in people alone. Family, and the ability to feed that family without destroying the environment or any other people, were the most important measure of wealth followed by friends, dependable ones who share dreams and work and skills and outlook, who brought in crops, drank each other's beer, laughed and cried, loved and forgave. A community of independent people living on their own individual plots of land, drawing on each other in times of fullness and hardship. This was a wealthy community.

But then I hear you cry, 'What about the hospitals and medical research and progress?' Well, that is a hard question to answer, but it would have seemed to John that a life lived on the land was worth a dozen lived off it, and the Bible measured a man's life in seventy years, not that much different from today, and moreover, seventy healthy years, seventy honest years, seventy years living on the land was a very noble way for a man or woman to live. John's final year is testament to this. Well over a hundred people came to his birthday party, even though John was too tired to get round them or spend a lot of time with them. All of them shared his goals for a new kind of culture - well, a very old kind of culture actually. And then his grave, natural in the earth, visited by his family is testament to the true worth of a man - not a bank manager in sight.

Then sigh not so,
But let them go,
And be you blithe and bonny,
Converting all your sounds of woe
Into. Hey, nonny, nonny.

Wm. Shakespeare
Much ado about Nothing

Selected books

John Seymour's writings have been his life work
from leaving the army after World War II. He
wrote forty books, and in his latter years was
working on a collection of autobiographical stories. His early work was a kind of three way conversation between John, his reader and a third person who may have been a ploughman, a fisherman,
a bushman, in fact anyone who interested John.
On the whole they were people, ordinary folk who
worked for a living. He had the knack of stamping
high ideals, almost gothic in conception, in to
words understood by the ordinary and unlearned.
Try as hard as he might, a writer might work for
all his life and only hope for the clarity that John
worked into his books.

Later John wrote about man in relation to his
environment. Quite simply his books championed
humanity first and foremost, the environment and
the rest of the planet second. He had, as the ink in
his pen, the idea that we could live on the earth,
grow fit and healthy young children, have happy
lives, almost in a utopian Eden, and still maintain
the health of the planet.

The Hard Way to India

Published by Eyre & Spottiswode 1951
This is a hugely interesting book, the story of a trip from London to Sri Lanka paid for by the BBC. John travels by train as far as Pakistan and then by plane over India.

Sailing Through England

Illustrations by Sally Seymour
Published by Eyre & Spottiswode in 1956
The tales of the journeys of Jenny the Third from the south coast along the channel and into the North Sea, and consequently into the waterways of East Anglia, Humberside and the canals of Yorkshire and Lancashire.

The Fat of the Land

Illustrations by Sally Seymour
Published by Faber 1961
The very first self-sufficiency book, and one which causes a change in direction for John's writing towards farming and self-sufficiency. John was becoming increasingly concerned with the way we live on the planet. The Fat of the Land was published again with extra material in 1974, and again with more extra material in 1991.

On My Own Terms
Published by Faber in 1963
A kind of autobiography in which the revised version was almost a completely new book. John said the first version was poor, and he didn't wonder that it didn't sell! The 1963 version has details of his youth which were removed in the 1980 version. Very interesting study of his life in Africa and the war.

Voyage into England
Published by David & Charles in 1966
The story of a barge journey through England that lasted for a year.

Willy-Nilly to the Baltic
Published 1968
John's journey in an open boat called Willy-nilly across the North Sea into the Baltic. John sailed from yacht club to yacht club, and was well received, telling stories, hearing tales and, of course, drinking a lot.

The Companion Guide to East Anglia
Published by Collins in 1970
The first of a series of guides to the geography, history, economics and, most importantly, the people of various English regions.

The Book of Boswell

Edited by John Seymour

Published by Gollancz in 1970.
A labour of love for John, who had a keen friendship with many Gypsies. This book is an important record in the English tradition of 'spoken word' biographies.

Self-Sufficiency

With Sally Seymour
Published by Faber in 1973
A more comprehensive look at the arts of self-sufficiency than found in The Fat of the Land, the precursor to the later books.

The Complete Book of Self-Sufficiency

Illustrations by Sally Seymour
Published by Dorling Kindersley in 1976
The book. It sold in hundreds of thousands and details in an almost step-by-step way, the life lived off the land. So many people call it their Bible. It contains 'how to' sections on nearly everything you would need to know about self-sufficiency, from growing vegetables to killing pigs.

Bring Me My Bow

Published by Turnstone Books in 1977
John at his prophetic and Blakean best - he argues for a better England and fondly marks the English character.

The Countryside Explained

Illustrations by Sally Seymour
Published by Faber in 1977
John relates conversations with old countrymen and explains the processes that have led to the countryside as we know it today. He is almost nostalgic for bygone days, but is clear in a call to get men and women involved back in the growing of our nation's food.

The Self-Sufficient Gardener

Illustrations by Sally Seymour
Published by Dorling Kindersley in 1978
The Complete Guide brought down to the gardening level. Many people living in urban areas can become largely self-sufficient.

John Seymour's Gardening Book

Published by A. Deutsch in 1978
It is difficult to realise that this book was published at the same time as the above book, but John was so popular an author. He invented this genre of books, the guide book to self-sufficiency, and it was copied many times. This was specifically designed to encourage younger gardeners.

I'm a Stranger here Myself
Published by Faber and Faber in 1978
The story of the family move from Orford to Pembroke-shire, farming in a different culture and with poor land and the beginnings of The Centre for Life.

Gardener's Delight
Published by M. Joseph in 1978
John writes of the folklore and history of growing vegeta-bles in the garden, as well as eating them in the kitchen.

The Lore of the Land
Illustrations by Sally Seymour
Published by Whittet Books in 1982
John's call to small is beautiful in relation to farming, and the proper husbandry of farms. Ownership of land being a misnomer, trusteeship a better way of looking at it.

Far from Paradise
with Herbert Giradet
Published by the BBC in 1986
The book of the television series where John travels through the world looking at the way people farm the land, pointing out ancient ways from his experiences in Africa and India, and hoping for a change in the way we relate to the land.

Blueprint for a Green Planet
with Herbert Giradet and Ian Penney
Published by Dorling Kindersley in 1987
A positive book about how individuals can change the future of the world by changing their own lifestyle. Facts about how bad things have become are interspersed by how we can do something about them, personally. A book of hope.

The Forgotten Household Crafts
Illustrated by Sally Seymour
Published by Dorling Kindersley in 1987
Our changing lifestyle has left us bereft of the knowledge that was once common, how to live by making our own. With this in mind, John tells us how to make butter, furniture, curtains and many other commodities.

The Ultimate Heresy
Published by Green Books in 1989
John argues that the environmental difficulties we face can be traced back to a heretical idea that humans are separate from the rest of nature, and that the spiritual re-joining of man and nature is an important goal in the planet's return to health.

Blessed Isle - One Man's Ireland
Published by Collins in 1992

A fantastic read. John struggles with himself and joins in head first with the culture that is Ireland. A comprehensive treatment of the way one nation can put down another, and a victorious picture of new found freedom and prosperity for the Irish people.

Retrieved from the Future
Published by New European Publications in 1996

A novel where the world is plunged into crisis by a lack of oil. John at his prophetic best and his faith in ordinary people to make the best of the world is touching.

Playing it for Laughs - a Book of Doggerel
Published by Metanoia Press in 1999

Poetry, funny, irreverent and hard hitting at times. John wrote on the cover that he was "completely prejudiced, utterly biased and without any sense of moderation or proportion." Not to be read by anyone under 84 and a half.

The New Complete Book of Self-Sufficiency
The Classic Guide for Realists and Dreamers
with Will Sutherland
Published by Dorling Kindersley in 2002

A reworking of the classic book with more pictures and extra sections.

The Self-Sufficient Life and How to Live It:

The Complete Back-to-Basics Guide

with Will Sutherland

Published by Dorling Kindersley in 2003

Living the Good Life and how to do it. Really a reworking of earlier books, but with a section on Distributism where John explains how living off the land builds communities and how this is the only viable future for man.

Abridged extract from
The Secret Life of Cows
Animal Sentience at Work
By Rosamund Young.

I have included a few extracts from Rosamund Young's book, 'The Secret Life of Cows.' The reason is that I feel that John would have agreed with what they are doing at Kite's Nest Farm. A farm that is almost totally self-sufficient.

Both the livestock and the land are free-range. The animals can roam over the woodland and meadows, seek shelter in barns or under hedgerows as they choose. Ancient woodland is kept intact and the meadows host rare plants no longer seen elsewhere in the UK. Their method of farming, a natural, traditional, more intimate method, allows Rosamund to know each animal as an individual and therefore to understand their characters, giving her an instinctive feeling 'when something is wrong.' Her unique observations have been recorded in this book.....

Mothers and Calves
Calves often make friends for life on the day they are born, or very soon after. Sometimes three calves all born within a short space of each other form a group but more often it is a two-calf friendship, usually between the two who are closest in age.

Relationships between mothers and calves are often more complicated and fascinating than those merely between peers. Some calves are boss over their mothers, some mothers are too protective and some too casual. But perhaps two of the more interesting stories concerned Dolly and Dolly 2 and Stephenie and Olivia. . .

Stephanie and her daughter Olivia enjoyed a normal, close relationship and went everywhere together until Olivia had her first calf. When the calf was due to be born, Stephanie advised and comforted Olivia and helped her choose a good spot to calve, close to clear, running water. Stephanie settled herself down at a handy but not intrusive distance. Olivia calved without difficulty and was immediately besotted by her beautiful cream-coloured bull calf whom we named Orlando. She licked him dry, suckled him and quite simple doted on him. Stephanie came along a couple of hours later to be introduced and for the next few days grazed nearby hoping to be a useful and integral part. As young calves spend a great deal of time sleeping in the first few days, grandmothers are often useful for babysitting.

Sometimes cows who are not related are called upon to babysit. It is quite common for one cow to look after several calves at once, but the job allocation is done democratically and cows take it in turns.

Sadly, Olivia did not want Stephanie's services. She did not wish to stir from Orlando's side. She ate as close to him as possible and whenever he moved she followed. She even refused her mother's offer of grooming; she ignored her shamefully. On the fourth day Stephanie's patience broke. Hurt and amazed she turned tail, jumped the nearest fence and went of into another field to graze with her erstwhile friends. To the best of my knowledge they never spoke to each other again.

The case of Dolly and her daughter was altogether different. Dolly was a wise, fairly old cow. She was dark mahogany, slim, neat and very, very clever. She had had many calves and had looked after each one superbly. She gave them four or five gallons of milk a day for several months, gradually reducing the amount over a twelve month period so that when the time came for them to be weaned they were deriving their basic diet from grass and hardly missed the milk. She groomed every inch every day. She protected and encouraged and told them all to be wary of human beings. 'They are not like us,' she told them. 'They have their uses, occasionally, but there is absolutely no obligation to fraternise.' They all heeded this advice.

Her first four calves were boys and they lived in magnificent isolation from, or more accurately, indifference to us. Dolly's fifth calf was a girl, Dolly 2.

Dolly 2 was very beautiful. She had big, deer-like eyes and a sweet and trusting nature. No matter what Old dolly said or did, young Dolly liked us and liked us to like her. Sometimes we felt encouraged to give Old Dolly a pat when we were stroking her calf, a sort of pat of congratulation. She would toss her head angrily as if we had forgotten the rules.

When Little Dolly was fifteen months old her mother had another calf and, true to previous form, devoted herself to it. Young Dolly was not spurned but was increasingly ignored and she understood that as an adult she must make her own friends and leave her mother to the job she was so good at.

When Young Dolly was getting close to having her first calf we looked at her every day and as the time got closer we went twice and then three times a day. We always try to be on hand in case we are needed although we seldom are. Each time she greeted us with friendly unconcern.

We were not there when Little Dolly decided to

calve. So far, nothing had ever gone wrong in her life and she did not expect it to. Instead of choosing an open, accessible place in which to calve, or walking home to ask us for help as several young cows had done before, she went as far away from home as she possibly could and settled down, hidden from all sides by hedges and hills.

When we discovered she had disappeared we knew why and began searching everywhere. There were five of us looking on that day and we all went in different directions with very specific orders.

Little Dolly was finally found behind a hill and she was a sad sight. The alarming truth was that in making a huge effort to produce, unaided, a much-too-big bull calf, Little Dolly had displaced her womb. The calf had been born dead, and when we found her, Little Dolly was lying down, exhausted. We set to work to try to ameliorate matters. While waiting for the vet to arrive we gave her a drink of water and covered her with a blanket. The vet arrived quickly and managed to reposition the womb. We then propped her up into a sitting position with bales of hay and straw and finally left her looking relatively comfortable but still tired and seemingly unable to stand.

When we went back to see her an hour later the blanket was in a heap on the grass, the bucket was empty and tipped over and Little Dolly was nowhere to be seen. We could not believe our eyes.

After much searching we found her three fields away, lying at the feet of her clever old mother being licked all over and comforted far more ably than we could ever have done.

We had not seen the two Dollys talking to each other for ages and just how Young Dolly knew where on the farm her mother would be we had no idea. We were glad to see that our policy of leaving gates open to allow all the stock to choose where to roam had been vindicated: at least Dolly's slow, staggering quest had not been thwarted by five-barred wooden barriers.

After six days of constant togetherness the Dollys parted again, happily, and went their own ways.

Cows make good Decisions

We have found over the years that if they are allowed the right conditions to live in, cattle make very good decisions. They need access at all times to shelter, pure water and good food, freedom from stress and a level of stability. If the weather forecast predicts rain but the cattle insist on staying out on the exposed pastures in mid-winter, or if in the middle of June with weather supposedly set fair, they come down to the barns and ask to be let in, we do well to take heed.

I have talked about the importance of ensuring that animals have permanent access to shelter. All sorts of structures can play a part in this requirement: trees, banks, walls and barns each have a role. However, the most important and versatile living shelter is a hedge.

The madness of removing hedgerows cannot be overstated. The many thousands of miles which have been destroyed have resulted in far more than the mere visual deprivation: gone too are roses of amber, white and several shades of pink cascading from the topmost boughs in May and June, resulting later in berries of every hue. Innumerable wild species rely on these. Birds have skyscraper dormitories and layered nesting sites not to mention their life-sustaining winter larder. A hedge that is old enough provides rosehip, plum, elderberry, crab apple, haw, nut, sloe, acorn, ash and honeysuckle berries. Timid creatures find safe havens, nipping easily through the barbed blackberry skirts to escape the fearless badger. Rabbits, dormice, and field voles all find their hidey-holes and the vulnerable ground-nesting birds have an enhanced chance of survival.

The decision making process animals are constantly involved in includes choosing exactly what to eat. Nibbling and browsing all sorts of different grasses, herbs, flowers, hedges and tree leaves gives them vital trace elements in their daily diet in the amounts they feel are appropriate; such decisions could not be made so effectively by us. The animals are all individuals.

Mass 'legislation' for the entire herd in terms of feed might suit the majority but we have always been concerned with minorities. It is not only more accurate and effective to let the animals decide, it is also cheaper. We have watched cows and sheep eat extraordinary plants in prodigious quantities. Cows will eat dark green, vicious-looking stinging nettles by the cubic yard and sheep often choose pointed, spikey thistle tops or tall, tough dock leaves, particularly after parturition when their energy reserves are depleted. And this is when they have access to good natural grass.

One particularly satisfying fact we have discovered is that if the animals have sustained an injury they like to eat quite large quantities of willow. We hope that this is connected to the origins of aspirin. If a willow tree is not growing in a handy place we cut and carry boughs to whoever needs it. Without exception they eat keenly, sometimes on several consecutive days. When they feel they no longer need it they will just walk away.

Farming Books and Videos Ltd

www.farmingbooksandvideos.com
www.theoutoftowncompany.co.uk

A Guide to Traditional Pig Keeping By Carol Harris
Traditional Cattle Breeds By Peter King
Spacious Days by Michael Twist
Hallowed Acres by Michael Twist
Glory Days by Michael Twist
Ireland - The Ducal Days by Michael Twist
Talking Sheepdogs by Derek Scrimgeour
An Introduction to Keeping Sheep By J. Upton and D. Soden
The Polytunnel Companion By Jayne Neville
The Shepherd's Pup (DVD) with Derek Scrimgeour
The Secret Life of Cows (Hardback) by Rosamund Young
The Secret Life of Cows (Paperback) by Rosamund Young
The Secret Life of the Farm (DVD) with Rosamund Young
You've Done What, My Lord? by Rory Clark
An English Country Manner by Rory Clark
One Dog and His Man by Marjorie Quarton

Jack and Friends
The Out of Town Story
By Paul Peacock

This book explores the whole 'Out of Town' phenomenon through the eyes of those who worked closely, both in front of the camera and behind it, with the hugely popular television presenter, Jack Hargreaves.
Due out April 2006
ISBN 1-904871-13-5